The **Altered** Landscape

The **Altered** Landscape

Edited by Peter E. Pool

Essays by Patricia Nelson Limerick,

Dave Hickey, *and* Thomas W. Southall

Published by the Nevada Museum of Art *in association with*   University of Nevada Press *Reno* • *Las Vegas*

University of Nevada Press, Reno, Nevada 89557 USA

Manufactured in Singapore

Library of Congress Cataloging-in-Publication Data

Nevada Museum of Art.

The altered landscape / edited by Peter E. Pool ; essays by Patricia Nelson

Limerick, Dave Hickey, and Thomas W. Southall.

p.   cm.

Includes bibliographical references.

ISBN 0-87417-330-2 (hardcover : alk. paper)

1. Landscape photography—United States. 2. Pool, Peter E., 1936–   .

3. Limerick, Patricia Nelson, 1951–   . 4. Hickey, Dave, 1940–   .

5. Southall, Thomas W., 1951–   . I. Title.

TR660.5.N467   1999   779'.367—dc21

98-43475

CIP

The paper used in this book meets the requirements of American

National Standard for Information Services—Permanence of Paper

for Printed Library Materials, ANSI Z39.48-1984. Binding materials were

selected for strength and durability.

Publication of this book was made possible through generous grants

received by The Nevada Museum of Art, including the Carol Franc Buck

Foundation, the National Endowment for the Arts, and the Nevada Arts

Council; and from Furthermore, the publication

program of the J. M. Kaplan Fund.

FIRST PRINTING

08   07   06   05   04   03   02   01   00   99   5   4   3   2   1

Dedicated to the memory of

CHELSEA MILLER GOIN,

artist, curator, academic, supporter of the arts.

Her spark culminated in this book.

CONTENTS

ILLUSTRATIONS

PLATES

merged into a collective sensibility that in many ways may define what the American West *will* become. These visions may only be clear when viewed through the lens of the twenty-first century, yet they have already begun to alter our understanding of the land on which we now live. These photographs serve as reminders that art has a crucial function in our society, and that artists' visions are intricately woven into our national psyche. As a testimony to the significance of landscape in our sense of ourselves and as evidence of our collective desire to live in harmony with the planet Earth, these visions mark a passage from the aesthetics and history of the nineteenth and twentieth centuries to the hopes, expectations, and fears of the next millennium.

Each artist's view of these issues follows a somewhat different trajectory. It is not the duty of the artist to integrate these various approaches. Rather, it is the duty of the critic, the institution, the curator to identify and unite the common threads, to create, *de novo,* a new and greater whole from the individual parts. That is the purpose of this collection. The common threads presented by the various artists in The Altered Landscape Collection come together in this volume, where they are addressed by Thomas W. Southall from an art-historical perspective, by Dave Hickey from an aesthetic perspective, and by Patricia Nelson Limerick from a social-historical perspective.

More and more, the ability of most museums to assemble a global collection of artistic movements has become a thing of the past, driven out by a vastly more complex world, limited resources for art, and the role of individual donors and the marketplace. A focused or signature collection provides an appropriate vehicle for the expression of a smaller museum's creative talents. The Nevada Museum of Art in Reno sits on a crossroad of the expanding West, the major site of this genre of photographic art. It thus became a natural site at which to develop a repository for this art.

This collection is indeed contemporary. All of the artists who comprise the core of the collection are living, and with rare exception, each was contacted relative to the works represented in the collection. In some cases, the artists provided unique ideas or insights into the collection, although they had no direct role in the selection process. Clearly, this relationship contributed to the organic whole of the collection, and the Museum is grateful indeed for their help.

The work of past artists provides important context for this collection. Although many who appreciate Ansel Adams's work see it as a perfect representation of extant nature, Adams manipulated his images in the darkroom to reproduce his own "previsualization" of the scene, his own sublime interpretation, not that presented by his subjects. For example, there is a historic tradition in the West that towns place their initials in chalk-white rock on a nearby mountain. In *Winter Sunrise, Sierra Nevada, from Lone Pine, California,* Ansel Adams physically removed the *LP* (representing Lone Pine) from his negative so the image would present a sublime rather than an "altered landscape" (fig. 1).[2] So different was Adams's view from that of The Altered Landscape artists that he created an "altered image."

The artists of The Altered Landscape tradition are certainly not the first to find interest in the structures that humans have imposed on nature. During the 1920s and 1930s, artists such as Margaret Bourke-White, Charles Sheeler, and Edward Weston made beautiful images of industrial plants. Their aim, however, was not to comment on the interaction of these man-made goliaths with the landscape, but rather to extol their form as an embodiment of beauty and to reinforce the identity of beauty with progress. In some cases, however, the choice was prescient. When Edward Weston captured a coffee cup in the desert (fig. 2) or a steam shovel overlooking a lake (fig. 3), his mood was one of amusement rather than commentary or involvement.[3] His attention was caught, his observations made, but the perspective was different. The intellectual stage had not been set. These were occasional observations, in the same genre as The Altered Landscape, but without the defining thread.

The concept of The Altered Landscape Collection, while springing from America and the American West, is being explored throughout the world. In the course of its natural evolution, this collection will be extended to include extraregional and inter-

FIGURE 2
Edward Weston, *"Hot Coffee," Mojave Desert.*
1937. Silverprint, 7.4 x 9.5 in., 18.8 x 24 cm.
Tucson, Edward Weston Archive, Center for
Creative Photography, University of Arizona.

national areas, ideas, and artists. The Altered Landscape is an issue of our times: less
and less can the land escape man; more and more man creates nature. "Human
tampering with the natural world has made Earth itself an artifact."[4]

The selection of artists and images for this collection has been, and continues to
be, made by a very directed process. In the first instance, the Museum collected artists
who were felt to represent the founding of this genre, artists whose work would have
inevitably entered the collection. Next, we added artists who have become major
figures in this area, and in many instances we made an effort to acquire whole bodies
of work. Subsequently, we extended the representation of artists to the "second
generation," adding to previously collected images further images to fill out bodies of
work. This process will continue. In addition, we are adding historically important
images, such as those of Ansel Adams and Edward Weston mentioned above, which
help to contextualize the collection. This process has led to a diverse group of artists
representing a wide range of ages, both sexes, and a variety of backgrounds, who

FIGURE 3

Edward Weston, *Steamshovel & Donner Lake*. 1937. Silverprint, 7.5 x 9.38 in., 19 x 23.82 cm. Tucson, Edward Weston Archive, Center for Creative Photography, University of Arizona.

bring with them a broad and bright vision of what it means to relate humankind and the environment in which we live.

This volume brings together the development of The Altered Landscape Collection with its context, its pioneering ideas, and its many branches that provide the direction for the future. The book is designed for both the beginner and the expert. It offers an opportunity to explore both modern landscape art and the interaction of art with our social fabric. The focus of this collection is on an artistic tradition only twenty years old. In that sense, readers should not think of the book as a retrospective but rather as a stage in an ongoing project. While the collection is unique in its focus, the future significance of its subject matter in the history of landscape art is far from determined. Our curatorial duty has been to frame this subject matter in a way that it can be judged in and by the future.

Peter E. Pool, Editor

The **Altered** Landscape

FIGURE 4

Peter de Lory, *We Rolled Through the West.* 1992. Silverprints; five panels, each 9.88 x 9.88 in., 25.1 x 25.1 cm.

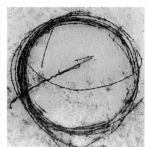

Paradise Altered Patricia Nelson Limerick

Alter (from the Latin for *other*): 1: to change; make different; modify.
2: to resew parts (of a garment) for a better fit. 3: (Dial.) to castrate.

The Photographer as Sphinx, Teacher, and Witness

Altered is a word of such enterprise, a word offering such thought-provoking twists and turns of definition, that one wants personally to thank all the unnamed folk who contributed to its development. Its use in the title of this book causes one to stop and contemplate it in a manner very similar to the way in which, stopping to look closely at a photograph, one surrenders the right to take it for granted.

Imagine a Classified Ads section, where authors describe the word they are looking for:

Wanted: Author seeks word for special assignment. The successful candidate must be brief, direct, and unpretentious, but also complex and resonant. This job requires a word strong enough to carry a complex and weighty burden of meaning in response to the question: "What on earth have two hundred years of American colonization done to the American West?" The word will have to hold its own in the company of powerful visual images, so it had better be tough.

The advertisement would bring out the usual candidates, and they would apply in their familiar teams of two. Even though the ad only asked for one word to fill the job, it has become hard, maybe even impossible, for these terms to work singly. What has American colonization done to the West? The West has been, the matched pairs of candidates respond, "degraded" and "improved"; "reduced" and "developed"; "devastated" and "settled"; "damaged" and "put to good use"; "raped" and "made profitable."

And, applying by itself, declaring that it is the one word that does not need a second word to help it do the job, comes the winning candidate. This flexible and hardworking word supplies three rich meanings for the price of one. After two hundred years of American colonization, the West has indeed been altered, in the sense of changed, made different, modified. In cheerful and positive terms, it has been reshaped and resewn in order to make a better fit to the needs and habits of the humans who have colonized it. And in the glummest of terms, the West has been castrated, neutered, and robbed of its power.

This is not your average word. With its three-way meaning, it gives its users at least momentary release from the pressure of choosing between the usual paired statements: (a) American colonization has made the West better, or (b) American colonization has made the West worse. To break out of that two-way choice, one must step back from the passion and momentum of the rapid transformation of the landscape and substitute terms of alteration and change for terms of improvement or decline. To a number of westerners today, such detachment is immoral, adding up to forfeiture and abandonment of responsibility for taking stands and action. If one steps back for a broader view, the enemy steps into the breach. Stop to think, and you surrender a few more inches of turf to the opposition. There are no time-outs in this rough sport. In the rushed, fast-forward pacing of western American history, moments of detached reflection have been rare—and risky. And yet, in ways that their viewers might both appreciate and resent, the photographs in this collection irritate us into exactly that sort of contemplation.

Can one celebrate and admire these photographers and still find much of their work irritating? You bet! A photograph can attract and appeal and still scrape and scratch at the viewer's mind. This abrasion of the mind occurs without the visual equivalent of shouting, arm-waving, or uproar on the artist's part. Agitation and photography do not mix. Maybe there are photographers who can shake with rage or jump up and down with pleasure while they do their work, but the result would seem guaranteed to be an unintelligible blur. Whatever agitation may come before and after the exposure of the film, taking a photograph requires the photographer to calm down, think, plan, and hold still—a discipline, regrettably, forced on few other professionals. That combination of intense feeling and a steady hand is a key to photography's power.

Thus, most of the photographs in The Altered Landscape Collection are tranquil and calm in tone; few of them shout or badger. But they irritate in the same manner in which a good teacher irritates students by refusing them packaged answers and by pressing them to reach their own conclusions and set the terms of their own understanding. "What are you telling us?" one says to these photographers. "What are you trying to persuade us to think about the scenes and conditions you record?" In the manner of the most unsettling and effective teachers, the photographers' works throw the questions back at their askers. "Figure it out for yourself," these images say to the viewer, and the viewer's immediate response may well be, "Thanks a lot!" Gratitude comes later. Sometimes, much later.

In my first two tries at writing essays to accompany exhibition catalogs, I spoke at length to the artists involved. In theory, I was writing about Mark Klett's photographs and Chuck Forsman's paintings, but I was also writing about Klett and Forsman themselves.[1] When the images wouldn't speak to me (or, more accurately, when I did not know whether the messages I thought I was getting were the messages I was supposed to be getting), I turned to the artists. When I couldn't figure out the images, I plagued both photographer and painter with questions: "What was your plan here? What did you mean? Why did you frame the view this way? What does this anthill, or this car, or this rock, or this dam, or this road stand for? Why did you put it in the picture?"

I took careful notes on their answers, and those notes gave me my orientation when I wrote the essays. This seemed like a good system, and I figured I had developed a new skill and a pretty workable technique. Then I went to speak at a midwestern liberal arts college, where, as part of my visit, I met with seniors who were writing honors theses in art history. When I quoted the self-explanations that the artists had given me, and quoted them very trustingly, the students' eyebrows went up. They were polite, but I had unmistakably demonstrated intellectual weakness, showing myself to be remarkably naïve. I actually thought that the artists could tell me what their work meant.

I write, this time, without any such taint. I have never met most of these artists, and I have not asked any of them what they think their work means. I have not quizzed them about their intentions and goals. I do not know what the word *altered* means or does not mean to them. I do not, for that matter, know their responses to any of the key words—*landscape, West, nature, human, improvement, decline.* I do not know what they think about dams, reservoirs, electricity, housing developments, rocks, petroglyphs, cars, or roads. When it comes to the artistic motivation and self-conception of the photographers here, my mind is an honorably blank slate. Attempting to match, at the least, the sophistication of graduating art history majors, I have reluctantly surrendered my naïve assumptions about the self-knowledge of artists.

And what reward has this earned me? In large part, anxiety. I have set up a fine opportunity to feel unmoored and unanchored. Without a record of the artists' words and thoughts to guide me, without any knowledge of their intentions and motives, I have come to know a little about how drivers feel when they start to descend a steep hill and realize that the brakes don't seem to be working. Opportunities for misinterpretation and misreading mark my road like sharp turns twisting along steep cliffs without guardrails. The steering, meanwhile, gives indications that it might be going the way of the brakes.

"What you are trying to tell me?" I say to the photographs, and in the manner of the best and most maddening teachers, they respond, "What do you think we're trying to tell you?" At that point, a great yearning for a tape recorder and a notepad, for the company, voices, and pleasantly misleading self-explanations of artists, comes over me. With those in hand, I could quote, paraphrase, and transmit these spoken messages to readers of this essay. But this is a level playing field, and my readers and I get off to an equal start. The photographer-as-sphinx speaks in riddles to us all. All we have to draw on are these visual variations on that magnificently ambiguous word *altered,* a word that shifts in its meanings as it turns in the light captured by cameras and film and preserved on the paper of this book.

Not all of the photographs are without words. The captions used by Peter Goin in his *Nuclear Landscapes* (fig. 5) series remind the viewer of the history and meaning of these places; the sites become all the more haunted with their explicit connection to nuclear weapons tests. Sharon Stewart's photographs of sites left polluted by industry are downright chatty. Toxic chemicals and their effects are, after all, not the

SEDAN CRATER

FIGURE 5

Peter Goin, *Sedan Crater,* from the series
Nuclear Landscapes: The Nevada Test Site. 1987.
Type-C print, 10.6 x 13.62 in., 26.7 x 34.6 cm.

easiest things to photograph. Landscapes that have never been host to chemical industries are perfectly capable of looking ragged and barren in their own natural ways, while lush plant growth and thriving animal life are not always discouraged by the presence of waste dumps. Thus, the text at the bottom of Stewart's photographs plays an important role in conveying the message of the creepiness of the places she looks at. In *Outfall Drainage Ditch at Union Carbide Plant* (pl. 61), an intestinal-looking pipe drains wastes from an industrial plant, sending chemicals off on a journey to the sea. Juxtaposed to the pipe, the printed statement that officials "have to find a balance of environmental and economic factors in the regulatory process" shows itself to be a pleasant-sounding promise already deep in default.

With her hospitality to words, Stewart has made an unusual choice for explicitness over implicitness, directness over subtlety, outright statement over evocation. She may well feel that the urgency of her cause makes open-endedness of meaning an unaffordable luxury. There is simply no time for the viewer to sit around wondering,

"What could Stewart possibly mean by this image?" While the leisured quest for her meaning proceeded, more and more toxic waste would have the opportunity to flow through more and more pipes into more and more rivers, lakes, and bays.

Look at the chain-link fence around the Union Carbide plant, think of the photographer's stance toward this site, and remember this urgency to communicate. Then think of the words from the Book of Job, words picked up and quoted by Herman Melville at the end of *Moby Dick*: "I only am alone escaped to tell thee." This statement makes a great deal of sense if you are the one clinging to the wreckage after Moby Dick has sunk the *Pequod*. It might make equal sense if you are the one standing outside a toxic waste site. Judging from the photograph alone, these chemicals could be very toxic indeed; no human life is visible. Everyone else may be dead or, at the least, on sick leave or disability. Somehow the photographer has made it past the fence and looked back to perceive and record the apparently lifeless Union Carbide plant.

The photographer, the image suggests, stands outside the fence, positioned to bear witness: "I only am alone escaped to tell thee." But who is the "thee" thus addressed, and where does that audience stand in relationship to this site? With that pipe taking what is inside the fence and moving it outside the fence, just how fully "escaped" can any witness be?

The West Turned Inside Out

Transferring a mess from one side of a fence to another, the Union Carbide pipe represents a very common breakdown in the calming and reassuring concepts of inside and outside. Water, air, soil, chemicals, and radioactivity have long been mobile, or are becoming more mobile over time. Defiance, rather than respect or submission, seems to characterize their stance toward the lines that try to divide inside from outside.

The walls of buildings represent the most easily recognized lines between the human sphere and the natural sphere, and yet some of the photographs in this collection question the firmness and steadiness of that phenomenon we call a "wall." A number of images show buildings under construction, with walls still in an early stage of skeletal framing. In Joe Deal's *Duplex Dividing Wall* (fig. 6), a couple of walls lie flat on the ground, waiting for their chance at verticality and meanwhile engaging in the improbable task of walling off the earth from the sky. Once constructed and teased into verticality, buildings can look substantial and hearty, planted for the ages. Masquerading as permanent shelter, the walls of buildings are actually settling down into their losing fight against gravity and entropy. Inside and outside are reaching for each other, trying hard to merge, willing the wall to get out of the way. In Michelle Van Parys's arresting *La-Z-Boy & Fireplace* (fig. 7), the walls have lost the fight. Released from confinement, a lounge chair and a fireplace sit congenially together in open land. This one-time house has been turned inside out, a fate awaiting any and every home on the planet.

FIGURE 11

Lewis Baltz, *#15,* from *The Nevada Portfolio*
(15 images). 1977. Silverprint, 6.38 x 9.5 in.,
16.2 x 24 cm.

outside and suggests that anything might happen in this luminous place: a prophet might come upon a vision; hope might get a new life; a new life might be conceived and born. Of course, it is a construction site; of course, it is an artifact of the despoliation of a more-or-less intact western landscape; of course, it is an imposition of sovereign, arrogant human will on the earth. The house is also quite a beautiful arrangement of line and light.

The West has been altered, adapted to a better fit with human activity, and one element of that adaptation is that the nights are a lot brighter. It is a great deal easier after sunset to read, write, cook, sew, and look at one another than it was a century ago. It is also possible, in activities unimaginable a century ago, to spend the evening watching television or using a computer. Dams, coal-fired plants, and nuclear power plants made this possible. And now some people tap into these omnipresent power lines, turn on their computers, and write impassioned denunciations of the injuries inflicted on the West by the production of cheap electrical power.

There is a small matter of inconsistency, perhaps hypocrisy, here. Many—perhaps all—of those who are most ardent today in condemning the crimes committed against nature by manipulative, domineering industrial civilization are themselves beneficiaries of that civilization and of many of those crimes. They rely on civilization's housing, its clothing, its camping equipment, its freeze-dried food packets, its cars, its highways, its airplanes, its light bulbs, its printing facilities, and its Internet. Civilization's transportation systems permit environmentalists to have the encounters with nature that transform their spirits and guide their politics. Civilization's information-distribution systems permit civilization's discontents to spread the word of their rage and to build their alliances of opposition. Grousing can occur because civilization nurtures, supports, and sometimes cheers for the grousers.

And yet asking civilization's discontents to give up their grousing, abandon their preferred language of lamentation, and adopt the neutral language of change, or "alteration," surely goes against the grain of human emotion. All the exercises of power recorded in these photographs, exercises in earth-moving, dam-building, house-constructing, road-making, and power-distributing have trashed landscapes that someone loved.

Say that something you value very much has just been run over by a truck. Let's say it was a hit-and-run truck that kept traveling on to a destination where the arrival of

cluster of toothpicks. The land is gullied and trashed; the water gives every indication of being charged with unhappy substances; the air and light are dirtied by emissions from the graceless plant. Okay, one could say, maybe the answer is that this wasn't the greatest place to begin with. The vegetation was probably scrubby to start with; there is nothing particularly appealing about the landforms. Before we could work up a good sense of loss and decline, we would have to be convinced that this site had something going for it in the first place.

But this photograph leaves little room for that kind of fudging. Put it in company with Robert Dawson's *Polluted New River* (fig. 16) and Martin Stupich's *Phelps Dodge Copper Pit* (pl. 63), and evasion comes to a halt. These places bring us back to that brutal third definition of *alter*—to the definition of altered landscapes as castrated landscapes. In these photographs, the potency of nature has been cut, severed, ripped off. At these sites, nature has been beaten, battered, mugged, lynched, savaged.

Things fall apart, William Butler Yeats said; the center cannot hold. These particular photographs suggest that Yeats got it right. And yet, in historical fact, the center has never held; things have always fallen apart.

The great consolation of the historian's life comes in the dozens of reminders one

FIGURE 15
Eric Paddock, *Louisiana-Pacific Waferboard Mill, Near Olathe, California.* 1989. Type-C print, 12.25 x 17.88 in., 31.1 x 45.42 cm.

FIGURE 16
Robert Dawson, *Polluted New River, Calexico,
Mexican American Border, California.* 1989.
Silverprint, 13.25 x 18 in., 33.6 x 45.7 cm.

receives that the past holds no golden age. Life today is a mess. Fortunately, life in the
past was also a mess. Late-twentieth-century environmentalists might dream of a time
in America's past when the neutering of nature had barely begun. They may yearn for
a time when the landscapes of the West were much less altered and thereby much
richer in the diversity of native plants and animals, with free-flowing, undammed
rivers, uncut forests, vast and unrestricted buffalo herds, plains and prairies rich with
native grasses. But for all these charms, life in nineteenth-century America was also
life with uncontrolled smallpox and cholera, slavery, murderous sectional conflict,
vicious wars between whites and Indians, and with absolutely nothing in the way of a
safety net for people facing misfortune or poverty.

Let me put this gently: those who see in the desecration of western nature a
ratification of the legend of the Fall, those who think that we are now living in
desperate and declined times, would find some relief for their terrible sense of loss if
they put down the newspaper and read a little history.

Nature's Magic Disappearing Act

The freshmen I teach now were born in 1977. Before they were born, the earth in these parts had moved a great deal, but significant units of western topsoil were staying put. Many of the West's present-day suburbs and resort communities weren't even a twinkle in developers' eyes. The earthmovers, the machines that reform the ground to make it receptive and accommodating to dams and roads and housing developments, had a lot of heavy lifting still to come.

Just as notably, before these students were born, North Americans of European descent were in possession of a firm and settled concept called "nature." Nature was a thing "out there," intact and set apart from human will and artifice. When left alone to arrive at its own balance, nature was steady and reliable. The harmony and balance of nature, the theory went, could teach profligate, impulsive human beings a good deal if they could clear out the arrogance blocking their channels of perception. If people could push beyond their vanity, untouched nature would give them a clear and orienting glimpse of the creative forces that shaped the planet. With that glimpse, humans could take their bearings and secure their moorings.

But how steady was nature? Winds, hurricanes, tornadoes, blizzards, droughts, floods, and earthquakes showed nature in moods other than the tranquil and harmonic. The widely accepted notion that, without human interference, ecosystems reached a climax state in which the species were arranged in the proper numbers, proportions, and relationships has yielded to a picture of nature always in change and flux. As historian William Cronon puts it, the natural world has been revealed to be "far more dynamic, far more changeable, and far more entangled with human history than popular beliefs about 'the balance of nature' have typically acknowledged." This changed understanding of nature, Cronon writes, "calls into question the familiar modern habit of appealing to nonhuman nature as the objective measure against which human uses of nature should be judged."[4]

As one of the most memorable examples of nature's instability, consider the Missouri River, famous in the nineteenth century for its tremendous momentum and power, its unruliness, its springtime abundance of mosquitoes, and especially its enthusiasm for undermining its banks. Loaded with branches, full of uprooted trees, and punctuated with treacherous sandbars, the river did not bring thoughts of the harmony and balance of nature into travelers' minds. And as boatmen struggled upriver, their journey was punctuated by unsettling roars and crashes when pieces and parts of the bank cascaded into the water.

In the late twentieth century, many environmental advocacy groups still hold to the conviction that untouched nature can provide human beings with a secure and stable footing, a refuge from uncertainty and turmoil. And yet the foundation for that faith has begun to imitate the banks of the Missouri River, collapsing, cascading, and crashing in a manner shaking to the nerves. Ecological investigations and scholarly studies have undermined the concept of a separate, intact, harmonic nature, until believers in that doctrine have the chance to learn what it is like to have the earth move under their feet.

North America was not pristine and untouched at the time of European colonization; the native peoples had hunted, farmed, started fires, and generally rearranged the topography for centuries. One of the preconditions for the creation of national parks as preserves of "untouched" nature was often the removal of the original human inhabitants. In the 1820s and the 1830s, fur trappers traveled all over the West, bringing beaver populations to the edge of extinction. Before the hide-hunters appeared, buffalo populations were already in a decline from competition with horses and from the impact of the Overland Trail. By the mid-nineteenth century, the human impact on nature in the West would seem to have been unmistakable.

But human imagination itself is an extraordinary power. Explorers, adventurers, tourists, pioneers, boosters, and promoters who wanted to see western nature as pristine, fresh from the hands of the Creator, simply went ahead and saw it in those terms. This task required categorizing the Native Americans as part of nature. With natives made kinfolk to animals, the long-term residence and habitation by indigenous peoples could be classified as "natural," and thereby their actions did not disrupt or taint nature in the manner of more certifiably "human" actions.

This casting of Native Americans as a part of nature, as a kind of animal, remains an attractive option for environmentalists trying to argue for the preservation of an intact nature. Consider this remarkable passage, first published in 1995, by western writer Rick Bass. These words appear in an essay lamenting the current battles over federal public-land management: "And caught in the crossfire—as they have been for over a hundred years—will be the grizzly and the trout, the elk and the wolf, the lynx and the wolverine. Waiting to join the ghosts of the American Indian, the buffalo, and the woodland caribou."[5]

There they go in their tragic march to extinction, the wild animals of pristine nature—the grizzly and the trout, the Indian and the buffalo. This willingness to dehumanize people is chilling, as is the premature obituary. Indian people altered landscapes; Indian people live today, declarations of ghastliness aside. But for the sake of creating a pure and pristine nature suitable for preservation, both their persistence and their humanity must be denied.

Nature was supposed to be the lodestone, the point of orientation, the baseline, the bedrock. And now, with its definitional disappearing act, nature is betraying its believers, pulling the rug out from under their most fundamental convictions. And if nature is going to pull tricks like this, then denial is the name of the game.

"We Would Have Healed Babylon, But She Is Not Healed"

In our premillennial times, we confront two Wests: the out-of-doors, wide-open-spaced, dirt-dominated rural West, and the enclosed-spaced, walled-off, indoors, asphalt-covered urban West. These can seem like the places where two different societies live, Arcadia and Babylon bordering up on each other and trying, not very successfully, to work out a mutually agreeable zoning code. The loudest voices from the rural West ask for the freedom to make a living from the land; they demand their right to continue to practice "traditional" land uses that are, in fact, barely a century old. The most audible requests from the city, meanwhile, ask for the rural West to be defined primarily as a place for urbanites to drive, hike, ski, ride mountain bikes, camp, romp, stay in bed-and-breakfasts, admire views, and recover from the pressures of life in the city. Babylon's more privileged and leisured residents have a vision and an agenda they intend to impose on Babylon's rural neighbors.

Rural people and urban people differ in a number of ways, and that difference shows up most clearly in their judgments of the right—and the wrong—ways to use natural resources. Just as clear—and closely related to their differences on land use—is the difference in the ways in which urban and rural people reckon with death. Rural people often know death as a familiar and immediate experience. Despite years of characterization as unsophisticated bumpkins, rural people have long had a head start in facing up to the rough realities of the ways in which living creatures arrive on and depart from the planet.

My father was raised on a farm in Brigham City, Utah. In the manner of rural youth, he faced the realities of life and death head-on. He hunted around the shores of the Great Salt Lake, killing birds for family dinners. His tasks sometimes included placing kittens in burlap bags and, in turn, placing those bags under water. There was a reason for this: the barn-cat species had exceeded its carrying capacity. Drowned kittens restored balance. For understandable reasons, my father had very mixed feelings toward the various kittens and cats of my childhood.

My father was a frequent patron of a hardware store and lumberyard in Calimesa, a few miles from our hometown of Banning. It was worth riding along on these trips, because this was also a feedstore and, in part, a pet store, with parakeets and chicks for sale. While there was no guarantee of success, accompanying Father to the hardware store and then expressing a desperate need for one of these little feathered items sometimes yielded results. The first result was a parakeet. The naming of the parakeet as "Elvis" should give a fairly accurate sense of the timing of this story.

On another visit, I was overcome by the cuteness of the baby chickens. My father agreed that I could have a couple. I took them home—and took them home in the same spirit with which I had taken home Elvis, thinking that I was adding to our pet population. The next week, in an evident flashback to his Brigham City childhood, my father decided that if we were going to have a couple of chickens, we might as well have enough to make it worthwhile. What, I should have asked, would "making it worthwhile" come to mean in practice? I did not ask; our pet and/or poultry holdings enlarged, and a dozen chicks came to live in the backyard.

With the passage of a few months, the chickens were pushing hard against the concept of "pet," sometimes breaking out of their jerry-rigged pen and running down 22nd Street, requiring energetic herding efforts to bring them back to a condition of official domestication. I was not familiar with the term *theodicy*; I had not yet struggled to understand, as the dictionary puts it, the reasons why "divine justice allows evil to exist." Chickens, however, brought that difficult concept within a child's reach. When it rained and the chickens got wet, the way they smelled was extraordinary. If chickens smelled like that, I asked my very religious grandmother, how, how could anyone believe in the goodness of God?

My sisters and I, however, still tried to hold on to our initial fondness for these chicks who had treacherously become chickens. My father, on the other hand, was an unreconstructed farmboy. And so the day came when he set up the chopping block, took up his ax, and showed us what that interesting phrase "to run around like a chicken with its head cut off" meant in practice.

While my father chopped off heads, my sisters and I wept and repeated our declaration that we would never eat our friends. If anyone in this household tried to serve us chicken, we said, we would go down the street to Ruth's Hamburger Stand. Where Ruth got her hamburger was a question we chose not to raise.

When our chickens had their heads cut off, they certainly seemed to be altered by the experience, though it would be hard to say that they were improved. But then, plucked, gutted, and dismembered, our pets turned out to be the centerpieces of wonderful dinners. They were meatier and certainly much richer in flavor than store-bought chickens. Loyalty made a full surrender to appetite. These chickens, after all, had proven remote, unaffectionate, and intractable in spirit; this was not the moral equivalent of eating Elvis. Still, I do not think we ever formally retracted the fevered statements we had made while the chickens hopped weirdly around the yard and our intractably rural father reminded his urban daughters of the easily evaded fact that what carnivores know as "dinner" was once fully alive.

To rural westerners, the opinions emanating from western cities today must sound like one prolonged chorus of the remarks we made to my father on that day. Here are these urbanites who, at their peak of down-to-earth productivity, grow some tomatoes and zucchini in their backyards. These people cannot feed themselves, cannot shelter themselves, cannot warm or light their own houses, without the help of a massive infrastructure. Worse, they do not even seem to know where all this food, shelter, warmth, and light come from. Milk comes in cartons, meat comes in plastic wrap, vegetables and fruit come washed and in bins, wood comes from lumberyards, and light and heat simply arrive when you turn on switches or activate thermostats.

At least these pathetically dependent urbanites could have the decency to say thank you. On the contrary, in the manner of my sisters and me in the backyard, they denounce their benefactors and weep over the injury inflicted on nature. They are stricken by the sufferings of animals and not much impressed or moved by the losses of displaced rural people. There is a chance that these fine-tuned urbanites would starve, or freeze, or spend their evenings sitting in the dark if they succeeded in imposing their standards on rural America. This prospect does not seem to trouble them.

The cities themselves have big troubles, troubles without clear solutions. Fracture lines of race and class run through the cities; educational and social-welfare institutions struggle for support and direction; and yet many privileged city-dwellers aim their energies and financial contributions away from the city's own problems and toward environmental groups that undertake to preserve "wilderness" areas where weary urbanites can restore their spirits and recharge their batteries. The residents of Babylon cannot heal Babylon, and yet they are full of plans and schemes to remake Babylon's rural surroundings. No wonder anxiety and anger are two of the principal products of the rural western economy at the end of the millennium.

The rules have changed, angry rural westerners complain. But the rules were never anything but changing. Western society and its arrangements prove to be as mobile, fluid, and dynamic as western nature and its arrangements. Rural westerners may be more aware of mortality in everyday life, but that does not make them any more enthusiastic about the possible death of their own way of life. Moorings and anchorages, sanctuary and refuge, permanence and security, are as hard to come by in Arcadia as they are in Babylon.

Saving the Planet

I was staying at a hotel in Reno, the home of The Altered Landscape Collection. Every time I used a towel, I experienced despair. There was a sign on the towel rack that said, You Can Save the Planet. I hoped this was true, but I suspected that it was not.

I was supposed to save the planet by indicating to the maid that I did not need to have my towels washed and changed every day. It is certainly true that I don't need my towels washed every day. I don't need to have my little soap bar thrown out every day, and I don't need to have a new wrapped bar put in its place. I don't need—I don't even want—any of this.

But I still don't think I will be able to save the planet.

The good news is that the planet may not need my help. Earth is a very big operation. It has already gone through cataclysms aplenty and extinctions galore, and it has recovered from them without help from me or anyone like me. If I and my fellow human beings continue our towel-washing, mess-making, post-Edenic ways, the planet will outlast us. Contemplate images like Peter de Lory's *Snake, Lightning, & Knife* (pl. 13), and one simply feels better. Even if it were lifeless, even if we weren't around to be impressed, Earth would still be a very impressive place.

We cannot save the planet, but the planet is incredibly gracious about continuing to save us. The aerial photography in this collection provides the best testimony to that persistent offer of salvation (pls. 6, 7, 9, 21, 30). These views of the surface of the earth from the perspective of the gods offer a repeated opportunity of redemption through wonder. The chance to view the earth from the sky is an astonishing privilege awarded us by the much-abused-and-abusing power of twentieth-century civilization. The sky, after all, was for millennia something human beings looked at, not from. We may sit, now, in airplanes as if we were blind, our curiosity focused on the question of how soon the plane will land and what we will do once landed. Thinking intently about this collection of photographs cures that blindness. On the flights I have taken recently, I have been drawn back to the window, and drawn back to the recognition that the most humdrum plane flight lets us see the planet as no human being could see it until this century.

The hypnotizing aerial photographs in this collection show the surface of the planet as a canvas marked by geological and biological forces and by acts of the human will. Viewed from the vantage point of the sky, the transformation of the world by patterns of electric light at night leaves one stunned and speechless. Viewed from above, roads become hieroglyphics carved into the earth (pl. 21). In their arbitrariness and cryptic logic, the roads become riddles written in dirt. They seem to be cosmic communications from a disordered mind. Disordered or not, the messages marked into the earth are communications, not from aliens, but from us.

Photography allows humans, at long last, to receive our own messages. Photographers permit us to pursue a conversation with ourselves. Talking to oneself is presumed by many to be a sign of mental illness, but when there is an urgent need for self-knowledge, then not talking to oneself is the greater sign of mental disease. The photographs in The Altered Landscape Collection permit us to respond to ourselves and to the messages we have marked into the earth. The photographers themselves do not pose as a detached and omniscient group of observers. They admit, instead, to being part of the species that does both the looking and the marking.

How will we save the planet? Let us, by all means, do all we can in the way of restrained towel-washing. Let us think intelligently about population growth and the strain that our habits of consumption put on natural resources and on our souls. Let us put energy and money into an intelligent cleanup of polluted sites. Let us reconsider our acts of dominance over earth, water, and air, and repent where we can. But let us do all this in the spirit opened to us by many of these photographs: a spirit of wonder, surprise, and gratitude that we are privileged to live on this planet, altered as it is. Let us savor the planet—and its residents—while we can.

Shooting the Land Dave Hickey

If we take Nature to mean natural simple instinct as opposed to self-conscious culture, the work produced under this influence is always old-fashioned, antiquated and out of date. . . . If, on the other hand, we regard Nature as a collection of phenomena external to man, people only discover in her what they bring to her. She has no suggestions of her own. Wordsworth went to the Lakes but he was never a lake poet. He found in stones the sermons he has already hidden there.
—Oscar Wilde

In the 1890s, when Oscar Wilde began insisting that life imitates art and that art designs nature—when he began chiding poets for going into nature and finding sermons in the stones—his remarks were dismissed as sophisticated phrase-making, as throwaway lines from an urban wit. The subsequent hundred years, however, would confirm Wilde's insight in spades, as the increasingly crowded, violent, and polycultural twentieth century made such relativism not only possible but necessary. In the 1950s, Claude Levi-Strauss would document its mechanics, demonstrating to all but the most obtuse that we live in a world of competing natures designed by competing cultures.

In practical terms, Wilde was simply suggesting that cultures portray their own nature, just as painters portray *their* own natures—that cultural constructions of nature bear the same relationship to the totality of the natural world that an artist's rendering does to the world before the eye. Since the totality of the natural world is always larger than our description of it and less inflected by our desires, Wilde felt that cultures expressed themselves through the *style* of nature they design and the medium out of which they construct it. Levi-Strauss would take this proposition one step further and argue that the design and construction of nature is the *main project* of culture—that every culture employs its arts and sciences to establish and maintain a "view" of the natural world that distinguishes nature from culture even as it invests that nature with its own absolute cultural values.

So, if life imitates art and art designs nature, the works of art and science in any particular culture must necessarily elaborate and reconfirm its own design of nature, or else propose some redesign of it, some "new" nature that will be visible in art long before we learn to recognize it in the natural world—if we ever do. Because this "new" nature will not "look natural" when we see it in art, we will presume that the problem is with the "art." Thus all quarrels about the nature of nature begin with quarrels about the nature of art, according to Wilde. So, when disparate and incommensurable views of the natural world begin competing within a single culture and within a single practice, there is every reason to suspect that received cultural ideas about the nature of nature are losing their authority, and this speaks to vaster cultural anxieties.

FIGURE 17
Frederic Edwin Church, *The Icebergs.* 1861.
Oil on canvas, 64.25 x 112.25 in.,
163.2 x 285.1 cm. Acc. 1979.28, anonymous
gift. Dallas, Dallas Museum of Art.

This, I would suggest, is demonstrably the case in the photographs in The Altered
Landscape Collection, an aggregation of images that, at first glance, seem anything
but anxious: just a collection of predominantly black-and-white photographs of the
natural world in the western United States in the late twentieth century—a selection
that tends to emphasize the primal landscape bereft of animals and vegetation, humans and the works of humans. For all their uniformity of format, medium, and
subject matter, however, these images present us with intellectual anomalies and visual
incommensurabilities that raise questions about the nature of photographic art, which
lead us directly to questions about our own culture's design of nature (figs. 17, 18, 19).

Not surprisingly, since this collection aspires to be representative, the larger portion of images in The Altered Landscape Collection tend to confirm and elaborate
the design of nature as we have imagined it since the Enlightenment. They represent
the look of nature in images informed by our dominant idea of it—as an emblem of
abiding beauty and sublimity: balanced, cyclical, and eternal. In order to do so, the
images of Robert Adams, Wanda Hammerbeck, Peter de Lory, and John Pfahl exploit
the formality and instantaneity of photographic images as metaphors for the eternal
balance of nature. They infer a representational relationship between the ahistorical
instant of the photograph and the ahistorical forever of eternity, as well as some
analogy between the formal balance of the rectangular image and the putative "balance of nature." To the same end, they employ the light-sensitivity of photography to
dramatize the *angle* of the light on the landscape as a signifier of nature's cycles—a
visual metaphor for its ahistorical temporality.

The revisionist portion of this collection, however, is informed by the suspicion

that the way we represent the landscape is somehow complicit in our exploitation of it. So these photographers aspire to portray nature differently and, in doing so, to portray another nature altogether—one born of the Atomic Age—a "one-way" nature that is as chaotic, dynamic, and historical as culture itself. To portray this "new" nature, then, photographers like Peter Goin, Richard Misrach, Lewis Baltz, and Patrick Nagatani seek to disengage the land from the landscape metaphors of modern photography.

They must break the metaphorical inference that binds the photographic "instant" to natural "eternity," the "formal picture" to the "balance of nature," the high-contrast glamour of "angled light" to the stability of "nature's cycles." And of course, since the frozen, formal, high-contrast, eternal picture constitutes the grail of modern art-photography, they must ultimately make bad or inappropriate art-photography in order to make good photographs of "one-way" historical nature. The question of whether this "new" nature is any more "real" than the "old" nature it seeks to supplant is, of course, one that Wilde would not deign to discuss, being content with the fact that it is undeniably more current.

The ascent to the heights of non-objective art is arduous and painful. But it is rewarding never-theless. The familiar begins to recede into the background. The contours of the objective world fade more and more, step by step, until finally the world—everything by which we have lived—becomes lost to sight. No more likeness of reality, no idealistic images—nothing but a desert.

I was fearful of leaving the ordinary world of will and idea, but the promise of liberation drew me onward—into a desert filled with the spirit of non-objective sensation—where nothing is real except feeling.
—Kasimir Malevich

Before embarking on a discussion of how these revisionists revise, however, it is important to step back and view the practice of all these photographers in terms of their commonality—to emphasize the fact that within the global history of representation, landscape photography is very much a local flavor—for even though all cultures construct a vision of nature, very few do so by making *pictures* of it. Traditional tribal cultures, for instance, tend to construct the natural world out of totems and pictographs grounded in invisible cultural antinomies—dialectical images and objects bereft of frames, pictorial syntax, and perspectival arrangement. Classical Mediterranean cultures, on the other hand, tend to embody nature in free-standing portrayals of its human and animal inhabitants, while orthodox Hebrew and Islamic cultures hold the natural world at arm's length, inscribing its construction in word and number without representing or embodying it.

The practice of describing nature by picturing the noncultural wilderness within a frame, from the perspective view of a human individual, however, is the specific, indigenous product of Northern Europe's Protestant diaspora after the dawn of the Enlightenment. Thus, despite the proliferation and ubiquity of landscape images in the western United States at the dead-end of this diaspora, we need to remember that the practice of picturing the landscape is rigorously bounded in time and space—and that the images in The Altered Landscape Collection, for all their ideological differences, are visions and revisions of an even more local, though no less influential, practice whose domain one may infer by driving southeast (as I have on occasion) from southern Nevada, across Arizona, New Mexico, and southern Texas into the Republic of Mexico.

If you dine in Mexican restaurants on this trip, as I do, and attend to the iconography that decorates their walls, the shifting languages of nature unfold before your eyes. In southern Nevada and northern Arizona, within the domain of Anglo culture, the decorations are invariably landscape pictures: brown hills, blue skies, white clouds, saguaro, maguey, and oleanders, with the occasional hacienda off in the distance, attended by primitivist cows. In eastern Arizona and central New Mexico, however, in Indian country, these landscapes are replaced by pictographs: Zuni sun signs, pastel thunderbirds, kachinas, and schematic corn shocks. The landscape image returns when you enter Texas, although with less vegetation, only to disappear once you cross the Rio Grande.

Upon entering the Republic of Mexico, the language of the land is replaced by the language of the body: Quetzalcoatl reigns, the eagle and the serpent struggle, the great bull swirls around the matador, and the Virgin of Guadalupe reveals herself to us, along with Aztec warriors, assorted *vaqueros,* Pancho Villa, and the occasional local saint. The landscape, however, is seen through Anglo eyes, so if you tarry long in Mexico you are inevitably overtaken by the vague sense of disorientation that arises from living among people who are not looking at the same things you are, or looking *for* the same things, or selecting out the same things as intrinsically meaningful.

We take the landscape with us wherever we go, in our eyes or as portable images, but the iconic image of the landscape remains ideologically specific to the traditions of Northern European Protestantism. Thus, as befits the art of a culture grounded in a personal religion of the visible Word, privately available on paper, the photographs in The Altered Landscape Collection emphasize the artist's personal, perspectival "view" of a Nature in which the visible Word (written in the "New Book of Nature") and the Flesh (of sinful, civilized, urban humans) are profoundly distinguished—so much so that the images of worldly, fleshly creatures like ourselves rarely sully the wild and vegetarian Nature of these landscape images. Why? Because, however abject, these landscapes represent a peaceable kingdom, bereft of predatory animals and men, free of harvest and slaughter—an edited text of Nature to be read with reference to the New Testament (figs. 20, 21).

More specifically, the photographs in The Altered Landscape Collection may be said to participate in the Puritan Modernist branch of this tradition. They portray aspects of the American countryside whose absence of atmospheric incident and decorative vegetation evokes Malevich's "desert of pure feeling" and allows the

FIGURE 20
Albert Bierstadt, *Sunset in the Yosemite Valley.*
1869. Oil on canvas, 35.75 x 52 in.,
90.2 x 132.1 cm. Stockton, Haggin Museum.

FIGURE 21
Albert Bierstadt, *Sunrise, Yosemite Valley.*
Ca. 1870. Oil on canvas, 36 x 52 in.,
91.4 x 132.1 cm. Acc. 1961.1. Fort Worth,
Amon Carter Museum.

landscape to mimic the reductive, formalist territories of European Modernism, upon which the works of industrial humans appear as decrepit blemishes on an equally abject (but essentially pure) armature of the primal design. Thus, in these images the radical distinction between the Word and the Flesh, which banishes men and women from the "lost Eden of the landscape," is further complicated by Protestantism's problematic relationship with the material world itself.

The emptiness that characterizes most contemporary images of the American

West, in fact, speaks as much of Anglo-Protestant alienation from the material world as it does of our awe at the spectacle of it. For we are not only *cultural* tourists in the New World, but *spiritual* tourists in the material world as well. Creatures of the eye, we read the world but rarely deign to caress it, and as a consequence the glass wall that the camera deploys between the body and the world, through which only the eye may pass, lends itself perfectly to our disembodied romance with the evacuated landscape that presents itself to us as a container for the spirit. The fact that this container of the eternal spirit is very often the historical container of eternal radioactivity simply does not signify in our quest for the desert of pure feeling, because it is the eternal, visual *idea* of nature that we worship in these images and not its harsh, historical facticity.

> *The charming landscape which I saw this morning is indubitably made up of some twenty or thirty farms. Miller owns this field, Locke that, and Manning the woodland beyond. But none of them owns the landscape. There is a property in the horizon which no man has but he whose eye can integrate it all, that is, the poet. This is the best part of these men's farms yet to this their warranty deed give no title.*
> —*Ralph Waldo Emerson*

It should be easy to portray the landscape of the American West in photographs, and it would be, were it not so easy to "take a picture" of it. To do that, we need only point and shoot (as the advertisements say)—and ask questions later, like the pioneers, gunslingers, surveyors, and test-site personnel who have come before us. So we do. We "shoot the land," bag our trophies, and take them home, although the landscape images we bag are less portrayals of the land than icons of its "spirit"—confirmations of the Apaches' suspicion that images steal the soul of their subjects. Because this is what we are doing—stealing the soul of the landscape for transportation to a more congenial environment for thoughtful contemplation.

Throughout its history, in fact, landscape picture-making has been less concerned with portraying the land in pictures than with taking pictures from it to document the taker's "personal vision," and this is especially so in the American West, whose pictoricality is presumed to be a public therapeutic resource. Consequently, the historical actuality of the land before the lens, its substantiality—the factual, historical condition of its serenity or abjection—has rarely been the subject of landscape photography, only the occasion for practicing it, and our experience of such pictures is less the product of the land before the lens than of the religio-ideological metaphors that bind landscape pictures to the idea of the American West and the aspirations of beaux-arts photography.

The revisionist images in The Altered Landscape Collection suggest that the time has finally come to shoot second and ask questions first, and the first question is: how does one portray the natural world in a picture when pictures of the natural world have themselves become naturalized, when nothing could be more natural, more ordinary, in the western United States in the late twentieth century, where such images constitute quotidian cultural artifacts, are very nearly *the* quotidian cultural artifacts? These images inhabit not just the walls of museums, but the walls of double-wide trailers and restaurants and the back walls of baptismals in Protestant churches.

Everywhere, the landscape picture prevails over the land: in recreational vehicles and tract homes, in Mission-style mansions and postmodern beach houses, in glass-and-steel corporate headquarters and behind the cash register at roadside filling stations. It lives in our gaze, which seeks it out, invited by "scenic overlooks," overlooked by balconies, framed by picture windows and windshields, simulated by city parks, playing fields, and golf courses. Even the cities of the American West seem designed and located to insist upon the primacy of that natural view, to dramatize the crinkled array of antediluvian mountains that is never far from sight in the Great American Desert.

Somewhere, wherever we are in Los Angeles or San Diego, in Las Vegas or Reno, in Phoenix or Tucson, Albuquerque or Santa Fe, Denver, Colorado Springs, or Salt Lake City, that jagged line of mountains lurks in the distance, inviting us, arguing with our animal natures—insisting so relentlessly upon the cultural signification of the natural world that we have come, almost inevitably, to think of the surface of the landscape image, the painting or the photograph, the *lens,* as a boundary marking the line between an alienated culture and a culturally meaningful nature that is lost to us, that we must necessarily long for and resent, whose natural purity we must aspire to, whose quotidian, historical substantiality we must consequently deny.

So the land gets lost in the landscape because, as Emerson shrewdly pointed out, the landscape never belongs to itself. The landscape, as created, belongs to God—is the Word of God, written in the Book of Nature. The actual property rights belong to private citizens or the government, and the landscape, *as seen,* belongs to us all, as poets of democracy. Its visual consumption is a sacramental rite in the American civil religion—our Eucharist as certainly as Nature is our church. So we collect emblems of our communion—not as images that portray a likeness to a real place, but as icons that embody a presence, as relics of the landscapes that we have acquired, have made pilgrimages to acquire and from which we have taken pictures, like ritual explorers or transcendental real-estate speculators.

What the cult image of a saint was to medieval Italians, what the Orthodox icon was to nineteenth-century Russians, or *santos* are to Catholic Latin Americans, the image of the landscape is to us. It is an embodied transhistorical presence. Thus, the documentary, historical function of any landscape image is always mitigated by the fact that such images are not only historical proofs but utopian promises as well—images of memory that are images of prophecy, too (Nature, of course, being presumed to be eternal). The whole tradition of nineteenth-century American landscape painting is grounded in this idea—in the assumption that, unlike European landscapes that portray the sites of *past* and *ongoing* history, American landscapes portray the sites upon which history would be played out *in the future* (figs. 22, 23).

Even today, Sierra Club ecologists market glamorous images of the landscape in

the same language that Renaissance clerics used to market images of Christ—as images poised between the secularity of the representation and the idolatry of the icon, as transhistorical *imagines,* representing a once and future reality. In Renaissance theology, such images were simultaneously a visual confirmation of the historical Christ and a promise of his return. In Sierra Club theology, images of natural grandeur function similarly as *imagines* of a once and future Eden, suppressing the local specificity and the factual historicity of the image.

The revisionist photographers in The Altered Landscape Collection, then, face two problems: first, they must somehow secularize a subject matter with complex religious overtones; and second, they must somehow redeem a practice whose formal and aesthetic "virtues" are heavily invested with those transhistorical religious overtones. So there is a kind of ecology at work here—an awareness of the shortcomings of photography's traditional virtues and a willingness to exploit them.

When these photographs fail to evoke the felicities of traditional landscape imagery, they fail self-consciously—or, failing that, they mimic these traditional compositions in such a way as to theatricalize their artificial relationship to their subject matter. Lewis Baltz and Richard Misrach, for instance, maintain the traditional "look" of the glamorous beaux-arts nature-picture while employing that pictorial eloquence as a signifier of irony and loss, creating exquisite, well-composed pictures of a landscape that is anything but balanced and eternal—a landscape despoiled by natural catastrophe, human depredation, exploitation, and other ephemeral intrusions, by test sites, brush fires, mining sites, septic tanks, trailers, and tract homes.

Patrick Nagatani, on the other hand, intrudes upon the Anglo-Protestant language of pictured nature with the nature-language of tribal and Oriental cultures, creating a kind of pidgin *bricolage* that infers the presence of a genuinely multicultural landscape—teasing the invisible language of western landscape into a kind of contested visibility by conflating it with the invisible cultural atmosphere of his totemic and pictographic images. Secondarily, Nagatani draws analogies between tribal iconography and the iconography of postatomic science that postdates the landscape tradition. The inference would seem to be, first, that Western culture has outgrown the landscape tradition, and second, that the language of pictographic iconography is better suited to evoke the radioactive atmosphere of invisible dread that informs the postnuclear countryside.

Peter Goin takes a third option in his photographs, reversing the strategy of Baltz and Misrach by dispensing with the "landscape picture" and its poise, drama, and balance, while retaining its classic subject matter in representative images that portray a "deformalized" landscape image whose anxious lack of completion insists upon the disjunction between image and the countryside it portrays. By photographing at high noon, Goin dispenses with the cyclical drama of angled light. By appending text and numbers (from another language of nature) to his images, he historicizes this subject matter and locates it "elsewhere" in time and space, somewhere beyond the "timelessness" of its portrayal. Occasionally, Goin infers historicity by doubling his images in a kind of extended time-lapse, juxtaposing photographs of the same place at different times, documenting the one-way historical permutation of the landscape—working in every case to undermine the iconicity of the "visible Word" and insisting upon its referentiality.

Finally, then, all of these revisionist images of the landscape seek to make a new kind of photograph in aid of a new image of nature—one that proposes itself as being more "true" to the "reality" of nature than the Romantic picture of nature that it strives to supplant. And they may, indeed, do so. Certainly, these revisionist images are more expressive of our current scientific view of nature than the icons of high modernity, but finally their truth value is moot. The important fact is that artists in this culture have begun to feel that our traditional image of nature is dangerously unresponsive to the needs of culture at this point in time, and compared to this overriding sense of cultural urgency, the relative "truth" or "reality" of these images is not only undemonstrable but finally beside the point. We make the nature that we need, and contest its efficacy in works of art. Nature itself, as Oscar Wilde assured us, has no suggestions of its own.

Where We Stand Thomas W. Southall

The images in The Altered Landscape Collection confront us with decaying cattle carcasses, sterile new homes in stark, unvegetated terrain, a sickly saguaro cactus riddled with bullet holes, bombing ranges and nuclear test sites, and numerous examples of mines, dams, and concrete that are impressive engineering feats but seem dramatically incongruous in their remote, unpopulated surroundings. Even the few images that don't show human-caused changes in the landscape, in particular Frank Gohlke's views of the aftermath of the Mount St. Helens volcanic eruption (pl. 22), depict a bleak and apparently dangerous world. Where are the glories of Yosemite, celebrated by a century of photographers from Carleton Watkins to Ansel Adams? Where are the inviting, bright colors of a New England autumn recorded by Eliot Porter?

Where a photographer stands can be critical to a photograph, both literally and figuratively. The vantage point where the photographer stands to position the camera and frame a subject can determine the composition and design of the resulting image. But where a photographer stands figuratively—how he or she feels about the subject and wants to present it—is equally critical to the meaning of the image and subsequently to how viewers might respond.

Photographs of beautiful landscapes can be deceptively transparent, encouraging viewers to relate to the inviting scene and treat the photograph as a surrogate for the experience of nature without being fully aware of the photographer's transformative and interpretive role. One of the attractions of photography, from its introduction in 1839, has been its uncannily convincing realism that almost magically transports viewers to remote landscapes they might otherwise never experience. In his famous mid-nineteenth-century essays, Oliver Wendell Holmes praised photography as a "mirror with a memory . . . a leaf from God's recording angel."[1] Another commentator, Jules Janin, said the photograph "is not a picture . . . it is the faithful memory of what man has built throughout the world and of landscapes everywhere. . . . You will write to Rome: Send me by post the dome of Saint Peter's and the dome of Saint Peter's will come to you by return mail."[2] This enthusiastic embrace of photography's surrogate realism has continued through the history of the medium and can still be seen in the latest fascination with computer-generated "virtual" reality.

The photographs made during the post–Civil War survey expeditions of the West provided practical documentation and mapping of the region's topography and resources, but they also allowed eager eastern viewers a surrogate experience of these strange, distant landscapes. This surrogate experience of the landscape continued strongly into the twentieth century, as many of us came to "know" Yosemite and other glorious scenery through the magnificent photography of Ansel Adams, not to

previously unseen landscape, now lost forever, along with similar Sierra Club publications helped raise the popular consciousness about the cost of unrestricted development and the thoughtless destruction of irreplaceable landscapes.

The photographs in The Altered Landscape Collection, made primarily in the last
two decades, reflect major departures from what we had come to expect of landscape
photography prior to the 1970s. The landscape subjects and photographic styles of
these contemporary workers are a far cry from the "straight" landscape aesthetic
exemplified in its most extreme by Ansel Adams's idealized views of pristine wilderness captured by dramatic rays of light seen under the most glorious conditions.
Instead of presenting a single alternative, this new generation of photographers offers
a wide diversity of both subjects and approaches. The artists in this collection are

united mainly by their departure from traditional romantic ideas of beauty, idealized wilderness, and the kinds of landscape that are worthy of consideration.

Although many photographs of crude mining, brutish engineering works, military destruction, sterile houses, and environmental destruction might seem overtly critical, most of these photographers' attitudes are not so obvious and can be as difficult to interpret as Watkins's beautiful views of destructive hydraulic mining. Rather than offer simplistic solutions, as did much of the crusading environmental work of the past, these Altered Landscape photographers pose more questions than they provide answers. The result of the contemporary work sampled in this collection has been to open up a lively new dialogue between the artistic, environmental, and general communities that encourages creative thought and reflection about how progress and preservation, people and nature, can coexist.

The preservation of wilderness is certainly a noble goal, but many photographers have come to realize that an idealized image of nature does not reflect our contemporary experience or needs. Even the celebration of natural beauty promoted by earlier photographers is now often met by many with a sense of sadness and loss, not pleasure. Robert Adams, the senior and perhaps the most influential photographer included in this collection, has written that "scenic grandeur is today sometimes painful. The beautiful places to which we journey for inspiration surprise us by the melancholy they can induce. . . . Our discouragement in the presence of beauty results, surely, from the way we have damaged the country, from what appears to be our inability now to stop, and from the fact that few of us can any longer hope to own a piece of undisturbed land."[3]

Many photographers and commentators now recognize that an idealized view of wilderness can be worse than an impossible goal—it can be self-defeating and potentially destructive to deny a presence or role for people in nature. If the only landscape we value is that which shows no human evidence, then we are placing ourselves apart from nature, paradoxically excluded from our own world.

Perhaps the leading advocate for a broader understanding of our relationship to the land, and a great influence on many of this new generation of photographers, has been J. B. Jackson, the founder and editor of the journal *Landscape* in the 1950s. His appreciation of the vernacular, occupied, and altered landscape demanded a new definition of landscape that accepted change and human interaction with the environment. Jackson and others offered new ways of looking at our towns, streets, gardens, and parks, and encouraged reconsideration of the very *concept* of landscape. He wrote, "It may be that I am on the track of that elusive landscape concept: the ideal landscape defined not as a static utopia dedicated to ecological or social or religious principles, but as an environment where permanence and change have struck a balance."[4]

The edges of civilization have become a central subject for many contemporary photographers. Robert Adams's understated views of tract homes along the Front

Range of the Colorado Rockies, revealed in a clear, gentle light by day and by their pattern of lights at night, subtly challenge us to consider how to make our homes and lives compatible with the land (fig. 27). In contrast, the newly constructed houses in the Nevada desert photographed by Lewis Baltz are radically depersonalized, without evidence of human occupation, looking more like sculpture than habitats (pl. 3). Eric Paddock's views of the creeping sprawl of civilization embody ironic twists, such as

an imploding molasses tank that suggests a new, humorous perspective on manmade disaster (pl. 56).

Numerous photographs in this collection warn us of the dangers of thoughtlessly altering the land, but the threat of a molasses flash flood is a playful way of reminding us that it is almost impossible to predict the problems we can create for ourselves. Peter Goin's rephotographic pairs documenting construction and changes around Lake Tahoe provide a historical perspective and a measurable record of the evolution of a highly managed natural landscape (pls. 24, 25). Our expectations of such before-and-after pairs might be to lament nature's loss to encroaching development, but Goin's photographs show that the pattern is much more complex: some obvious losses, some compatible changes, even some improvements.

The concerns and approaches of these photographers are widely varied, but they draw our attention to the everyday world we have created and live in, not the uncommon spectacular environment of a national park where nature is preserved like a zoo for occasional visits. As Frank Gohlke has argued, "where we live is far more important than where we visit."[5]

Building on the artistic freedom established in recent decades, many photographers have employed a diversity of media and approaches that significantly departs from the confines of the "straight" modernist aesthetic typified by earlier landscape masters such as Edward Weston, Ansel Adams, and Alfred Stieglitz. Three decades ago, Eliot Porter was virtually the only serious landscape photographer working in color; now almost half the photographers in this collection use color materials. Many recent photographers employ overtly self-conscious styles and techniques that call attention to the photographic process and, in doing so, deny the transparent realism of many earlier photographs that allowed, even encouraged, viewers to relate directly to the landscape subject itself and to treat the photograph as a substitute for the experience of the landscape. Peter de Lory, for example, uses straight black-and-white technique, but his sequencing of images of a hay bale, cut tree trunk, and automobile tire (fig. 4) makes viewers consider the metaphoric relationship between these diverse altered subjects, not the objects themselves.

Patrick Nagatani's frankly staged tableaus reflect an awareness that many of the important issues that concern artists today are difficult, if not impossible, to express in a straight photograph. His obvious montaged studio constructions depict the Trinity Site of the first atomic bomb test seen behind a constructed screen of floating fallout (fig. 28). Another of his images superimposes a floating Kweo/Wolf kachina in front of a uranium tailings spill dotted by bloated animal carcasses (pl. 51). In these and other images, Nagatani uses overt manipulation to represent invisible effects and cultural interactions that could not be represented in a single straight image.

Nagatani and others often accompany their photographs with extensive text. Some, like Peter Goin, Mark Klett, and Sharon Stewart, bluntly incorporate these

FIGURE 28
Patrick Nagatani, *Trinitite, Ground Zero, Trinity Site, New Mexico* (collaborated in part with Andree Tracey). 1988–89. Chromogenic color print, 17 x 22.75 in., 43.2 x 57.78 cm.

texts into their images in ways that would be anathema to the purist aesthetic of many earlier "fine art" photographers. Klett's handwritten notes have the effect of a personalized diary and recall the descriptive printed-in titles of many nineteenth-century topographic photographers. Goin's short titles printed into his "Nuclear Landscape" images are in block letters with slightly blurred edges suggesting radioactive contamination. This visual metaphor of radiation, as much as the descriptive identification, transforms what otherwise might seem a benign landscape and gives tangible expression to the often invisible but deadly presence of pollution and radioactive contamination. Stewart accompanies her images with even more extensive text presenting conflicting and contradictory statements about the subject from various sources, such as industry, government officials, environmentalists, and common citizens.

John Pfahl's work even parodies traditional landscape aesthetics through numerous references to earlier artists. His visual pun on the similarities between the surf and a strip of lace he has laid across the foreground spoofs the overly reverential approach of Ansel Adams's classic view of Pacific surf, but at the same time, in his own tongue-in-cheek way, Pfahl still celebrates the sensual beauty of nature and its photographed image (fig. 29). By freely altering a scene, Pfahl reminds us how far we have come from the 1930s, when Edward Weston was soundly challenged by his photographic colleagues for "staging" a photograph by placing a shell on a rock (fig. 30).

While many photographers have enthusiastically adopted experimental techniques and overt manipulation, even more have adopted subtler, understated ways of representing the land. This new approach to landscape imagery was first highlighted in the seminal 1975 George Eastman House exhibition, *New Topographics: Photographs of a Man-Altered Landscape,* which featured many of the photographers in this collection, including Robert Adams, Lewis Baltz, Joe Deal, and Frank Gohlke. Although that

FIGURE 29
John Pfahl, *Wave, Lave, Lace (Pescadero Beach, California, March 1978).* 1978. Dye transfer print, 14.25 x 18.19 in., 36.2 x 46.2 cm.

FIGURE 30
Edward Weston, *Shell and Rock Arrangement*.
1931. Silverprint, 7.5 x 9.4 in., 19 x 23.9 cm.
Tucson, Center for Creative Photography.

exhibition, like The Altered Landscape Collection, included too many different concerns and sensibilities to be satisfactorily grouped under one heading, most of these photographers were united in trying to downplay personal style and explore what William Jenkins, curator of the *New Topographics* exhibition, called a "non-judgmental"[6] approach to landscape imagery. It may be an impossible artistic conceit to eliminate personal style—the basic act of selection ensures a subjective point of view and style— but minimizing personal style centers our attention on the land rather than on the photographers' interpretation and expressive style. This may be unsettling for viewers who are not so obviously guided and controlled, but it also can lead to greater complexity that better reflects the dilemma of how we can both use and preserve our world.

The diversity of styles and concerns evident in The Altered Landscape Collection is a reflection of new connections and a removal of barriers between media, not just the insular world of art photography. Photography's liberation from its long-held artistic status as second-rank outcast and its subsequent defensive isolation has led to a lively exchange in media and aesthetics. Just as the Depression-era documentary photographs of our commercial environment helped provide a foundation for the pop-art and photo-realism movements of the 1960s and 1970s, those painters in turn contributed to recent photographers' appreciation of our vernacular environment. John Pfahl's "Altered Landscape" series has obvious affinities with conceptual art and earthworks in his emphasis on ideas and free manipulation of the landscape itself, but his continued commitment to the formal values of the photographic print never relegates the photograph to the role of a mere secondary record.

The connections between these recent photographs and earthworks are especially rich. The earthworks of Robert Smithson, Michael Heizer, and numerous other artists, which were based on an actual physical involvement with the land outside of the confines of the art museum, may have been the most innovative response to landscape ideas in the second half of this century (fig. 31). The earthwork artists' attention to common, otherwise unconsidered landscapes and the way we mark and modify them provided an important model for recent photographers, which was especially underscored by the artists' active use of photography to record their remote constructions. Numerous artists recognized that photographs were an effective, even essential means of documenting, communicating, and preserving earthworks that were often remote and intentionally transitory. Although most earthwork photographs were intentionally understated descriptive records—certainly a far cry from the "fine art" printing and aesthetics of traditional landscape photography—the directness of record photographs by Smithson and others have clear parallels in the work in *New Topographics* and numerous later photographs by such artists as Lewis Baltz, John Pfahl, Joe Deal, and Sharon Stewart. It hardly matters if these photographers were inspired by or are making conscious references to earthworks, because viewers will bring these associations to the work. It is difficult to look at Sant Khalsa's photograph of a dam site (pl. 40), Martin Stupich's view of the Phelps Dodge open-pit copper mine (pl. 63), Robert Dawson's view of a concrete irrigation canal (pl. 12), or Marilyn Bridges's aerial view of prehistoric markings (fig. 32) without thinking of them as earthworks created by unknown engineer/artists.

The new aesthetic freedom of the last few decades has also resulted in very different expectations for the photograph as a social and political tool. The recent photographers in this collection are all of a generation that matured along with the ecology movement and are aware of and in most cases supportive of environmental politics, but they do not necessarily see their art as the appropriate or effective vehicle for expressing political beliefs. Some, such as Peter Goin, Robert Dawson, and Sharon Stewart, have tried to take a more politically active role by presenting their photographs in popular forums beyond art galleries and museums. Stewart's photographs

Michael Heizer, *Double Negative, Virgin River Mesa, Nevada.* 1969–71. Silverprint, documentation of land project, 1500 x 50 x 30 ft., 457.5 x 15.25 x 9.2 m.

Marilyn Bridges, *Parker Rattlesnake, Arizona.* 1983. Silverprint, 10 x 12.75 in., 25.4 x 32.38 cm.

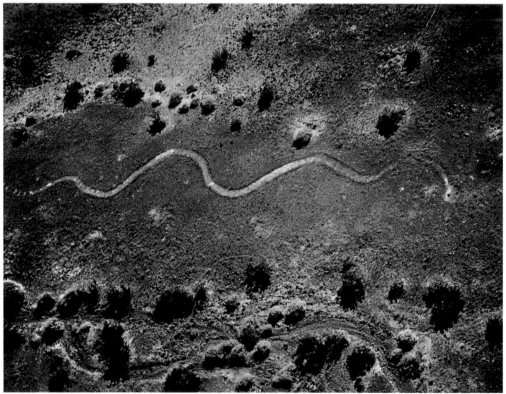

may present the multiple perspectives of industrial developers and environmentalists, but her images and her presentation of damaged landscapes make it pretty clear where her sympathies lie. It would be hard to mistake the bitter irony and frank sense of loss and criticism evident in the titling of Wanda Hammerbeck's images, such as the fenced-off Yellowstone geyser ironically titled *The Rights of Nature* (pl. 32).

For the most part, however, these photographers do not see their photography as an instrument for political action. Terry Evans, for example, asserts, "I am not a lobbyist. I am an artist-photographer who is passionately committed to social and environmental issues."[7] John Pfahl perhaps best represents the challenging ambiguity that runs through this collection when he chooses complexity over simple polemics: "I'm not interested in pushing simple opinions or making propagandistic statements. It seems to me that when more than one message is presented in a work of art, a tension is created that cries out for resolution."[8]

Ultimately, the strength and meaning of this collection is its diversity of approaches and opinions. Rather than offer one simple solution, these images instead suggest the complexity of the problems and the need to address them. Most photographers are presented in this collection by enough examples to give us a suggestion of their individual goals and concerns, but it is the contrasts between the different photographers that become most striking and enlightening.

It is appropriate that many photographs share similar subject matter, so that even a common hay bale can be seen in different ways, from Peter de Lory's view emphasizing the round pattern created by harvesting (fig. 4), to Eric Paddock's more utilitarian scene of a lonely bale on the road in the back of a pickup (pl. 55), to Terry Evans's aerial view capturing bales distributed across a farm landscape (pl. 19). Mark Klett's photograph of a hill marked with a calligraphic bike loop is an understated, almost humorous document of an irreverent insensitivity to the land (fig. 33). However, when tire tracks are multiplied in Robert Adams's view of a quarried mesa (fig. 34), we see the connection between our actions and responsibilities as individuals magnified by group and corporate action. Neither is inherently bad or destructive, but also neither is inherently benign or innocent.

Joe Deal's photograph of people jumbled on a graffiti-covered rock (pl. 15) provides a humorous complement and an additional layer of meaning to Lawrence McFarland's photographs of Indian rock art (pls. 46, 47). We retain the mystery and sacred quality that imbues this and other McFarland photographs, but the juxtaposition to Deal's work also makes it seem less remote and not so different from today's activities, while McFarland's photograph in turn makes Deal's seem less disrespectful. The contrast between the sacred and the secular or even profane is further echoed in the aerial views of ancient earth drawings documented by Marilyn Bridges (fig. 35), compared to the elaborate pattern of a bombing site photographed by Terry Evans (pl. 20). In both cases, the photographers are showing us altered landscapes that transform the landscape into a display for very different viewers and purposes. The spirituality of the ancient earth-writing, which may have been intended for some unseen deity, challenges us to consider the intended and unintended messages conveyed by Evans's contemporary military subject.

If we are disposed to be impressed by human engineering and the ability to manipulate the environment, Sant Khalsa, Robert Dawson, Martin Stupich, and

FIGURE 33
Mark Klett, *Dirt-Bike Loop West of Hanksville, Utah, 4/18/91*. 1991. Silverprint, 16 x 20 in., 40.6 x 50.8 cm.

FIGURE 34
Robert Adams, *Quarried Mesa Top, Pueblo County, Colorado*. 1978. Silverprint, 8.88 x 11 in., 22.55 x 27.9 cm.

FIGURE 35

Marilyn Bridges, *Winterhaven-Stickman, California*. 1983. Silverprint, 10 x 12.88 in., 25.4 x 32.72 cm.

numerous others provide a wealth of beautifully rendered images of monumental engineering projects. But when seen in juxtaposition with so many other more modest, smaller-scale changes in the land, these magnificent works seem brutish, arrogant, and insensitive. In contrast to the huge dams and engineering projects, Len Jenshel's photograph of a small puddle of water at the head of a desert drain makes precious what the other photographs make seem abundant (fig. 36). Through single images like Jenshel's and the juxtaposition of different photographers' works, the cumulative effect of the collection tends to personalize and individualize issues about our relationship to the land.

The range of landscapes depicted in this collection demonstrates that alteration takes many different forms: from volcanic eruptions caused by the power of nature alone to countless human alterations of various scales, from modest paths to gigantic dams, from the invisible effects of pollution and radiation to synthetic studio constructions. This variety of change, and of ways to represent it, calls for a positive stance to

FIGURE 36

Len Jenshel, *Death Valley National Monument, California.* 1987. Type-C print, 14.75 x 21.88 in., 37.5 x 55.58 cm.

confront alterations in our environment. Many of these photographs suggest that change can be healthy, even necessary, if considered thoughtfully with a recognition of its consequences. These photographs demonstrate that change and alteration must not only be seen as loss and destruction, but can also mean life and survival. On the other hand, deluded ideals that exclude change and human activity may not result in preservation but in a static death.

Traditional landscape photographers may have given us false comfort by creating an artificially secure and oversimplified relationship with the land, but these contemporary photographers, in contrast, present an unsettling series of unanswered questions. If such complexity and ambiguity result in serious reflection, this will be the most important contribution of recent landscape photography. These photographs challenge our traditional ideas of beauty and pleasure, but they also transcend simplistic lamentations about loss and ultimately suggest greater optimism about the future and the role we can play. J. B. Jackson wrote that "mobility and change are the key to the vernacular landscape, but of an involuntary, reluctant sort; not the expression of restlessness and search for improvement but an unending patient adjustment to circumstances."[9]

The final critical issue of where we *stand* is beyond matters of composition and different interpretations. These photographs also help us become aware of where we *stand at this particular point in time,* where we have been and what our options might be for the future. If these photographs help us to accept and understand our need to change along with our environment in a thoughtful, moderated way, then they have accomplished more than we should ever expect of either art or propaganda.

Plates

PLATE 1
Robert Adams, *Dead Palms Partially Uprooted, Ontario, California.* 1983.
Silverprint, 8.88 x 11.12 in., 22.55 x 28.24 cm.

PLATE 2
Robert Adams, *Burning Oil Sludge, Boulder County, Colorado.* 1974.
Silverprint, 5.88 x 7.5 in., 14.94 x 19 cm.

54

PLATE 4 Barbara Bosworth, *Nate, Skinning Day, Moosehead Lake, Maine.* 1992. Silverprint, 17.12 x 13.56 in., 43.48 x 34.44 cm.

Barbara Bosworth, *Moose Meat, Pittsburgh, New Hampshire.* 1992.
Silverprint, 13.5 x 17 in., 34.3 x 43.2 cm.

PLATE 6
Marilyn Bridges, *Highway Emerging, Nevada.* 1991.
Silverprint, 10.19 x 13.12 in., 25.88 x 33.32 cm.

61

PLATE 9
Robert Dawson, *Oildale, California.* 1985.
Silverprint, 14.4 x 18 in., 36.6 x 45.7 cm.

64

PLATE 10
Robert Dawson, *Private Property, Lake Tahoe, California.* 1988.
Silverprint, 14 x 18.1 in., 35.6 x 46 cm.

PLATE 12

Robert Dawson, *San Luis Drain, Kesterson National Wildlife Refuge, California.* 1985.
Silverprint, 14 x 18 in., 35.6 x 45.7 cm.

PLATE 13

Peter de Lory, *Snake, Lightning & Knife.* 1989.

Silverprint, triptych. *Snake, Lightning:* 15 x 17.88 in., 38.1 x 45.4 cm.; *Knife:* 14.88 x 14.88 in., 37.8 x 37.8 cm.

PLATE 14

Joe Deal, *Santa Ana Winds, Riverside, California*. 1983.

Silverprint, 11 x 14 in., 27.9 x 35.5 cm.

PLATE 15
Joe Deal, *Retreat, Upland, California.* 1983.
Silverprint, 11 x 14 in., 27.9 x 35.5 cm.

PLATE 16

Joe Deal, *Sunset Beach, California.* 1978.

Silverprint, 11.12 x 11.19 in., 28.24 x 28.42 cm.

PLATE 17
Robert Del Tredici, *Tending to Misty Rain (Area 12, Nevada Test Site, Nye County, Nevada, October 29, 1984)*. 1984.
Silverprint, 12.25 x 18.12 in., 31.1 x 46 cm.

PLATE 18
Robert Del Tredici, *Industrial Safety Sign (Area 5, Nevada Test Site, Mercury, Nevada, July 1983)*. 1983.
Silverprint, 12.25 x 18.12 in., 31.1 x 46 cm.

PLATE 19
Terry Evans, *Haystacks, South Central Nebraska.* 1990.
Silverprint, 14.75 x 14.5 in., 37.5 x 36.8 cm.

PLATE·21

Frank Gohlke, *Aerial View, Clearcuts and Logging Roads Outside Impact Area—Approximately 20 Miles West of Mount St. Helens, Washington.* 1982.
Silverprint, 14.5 x 17.5 in., 36.8 x 44.4 cm.

76

PLATE 22

Frank Gohlke, *Valley of Clearwater Creek, Salvage and Replanting Completed, Trees Left Standing
to Provide Wildlife Habitat—10 Miles NE of Mt. St. Helens, Washington.* 1983.
Silverprint, 7.38 x 22.62 in., 18.74 x 57.45 cm.

PLATE 23
Frank Gohlke, *Regrowth in Valley of Clearwater Creek—10 Miles NE of Mount St. Helens.* 1990.
Silverprint, 7.44 x 22.75 in., 18.9 x 57.8 cm.

PLATE 24

Peter Goin, *Donner Lake (from Donner Pass),* from the series *Stopping Time: A Rephotographic Survey of Lake Tahoe.* 1992. Historical photograph courtesy of North Lake Tahoe Historical Society, Tahoe City, California. Silverprint, each 10.5 x 13.5 in., 26.7 x 34.3 cm.

PLATE 25
Peter Goin, *Stateline, Nevada,*
from the series *Stopping Time:*
A Rephotographic Survey of Lake
Tahoe. 1992. Historical
photograph courtesy of
Nevada Historical Society,
Reno, Nevada. Silverprint,
each 10.5 x 13.5 in.,
26.7 x 34.3 cm.

PLATE 26
Peter Goin, *Railroad Trestle,* from the series *Nuclear Landscapes: The Nevada Test Site.* 1987.
Type-C print, 10.5 x 13.5 in., 26.7 x 34.3 cm.

PLATE 27
Peter Goin, *Enclosed and Electrified Fence,* from the series *Nuclear Landscapes: The Nevada Test Site.* 1987.
Type-C print, 10.5 x 13.5 in., 26.7 x 34.3 cm.

PLATE 28

Peter Goin, *How Would a House Withstand Nuclear Wind?* from the series *Nuclear Landscapes: The Nevada Test Site.* 1987.
Type-C print, 10.5 x 13.5 in., 26.7 x 34.3 cm.

PLATE 29

Peter Goin, *Destroyed Road and Crater,* from the series *Nuclear Landscapes: The Nevada Test Site.* 1987.
Type-C print, 10.5 x 13.5 in., 26.7 x 34.3 cm.

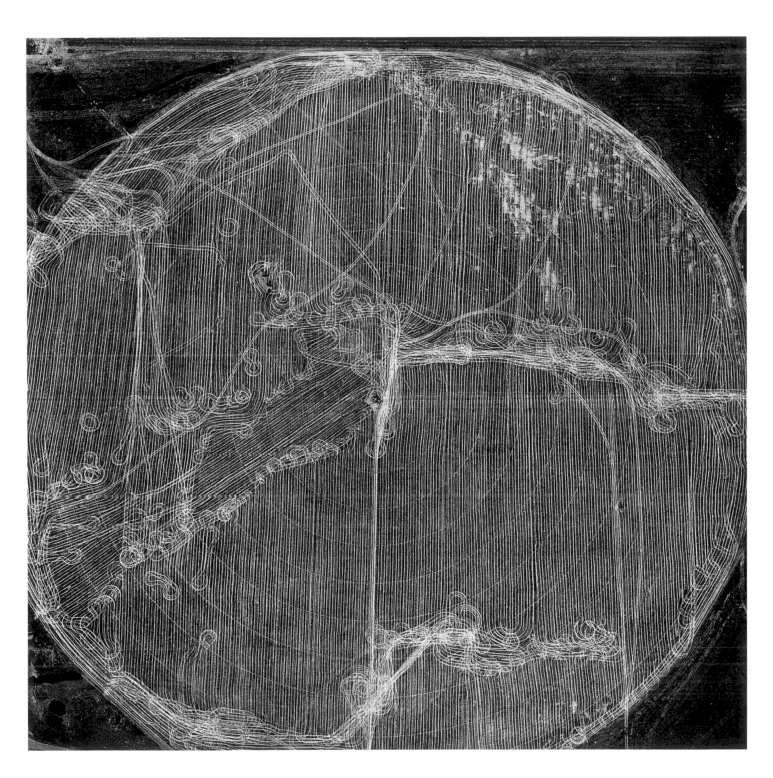

PLATE 30

Emmet Gowin, *Pivot Agriculture, Washington.* 1987.

Toned silver gelatin print, 9.62 x 9.5 in., 24.43 x 24 cm.

ARCHITECTURE INFORMED BY LAND

PLATE 31
Wanda Hammerbeck, *Architecture Informed by Land.* 1992.
Type-C print, 16 x 23.25 in., 40.6 x 59 cm.

THE RIGHTS OF NATURE

PLATE 32
Wanda Hammerbeck, *The Rights of Nature.* 1993.
Type-C print, 16 x 23.25 in., 40.6 x 59 cm.

PLATE 37

Len Jenshel, *Great Basin National Park, Nevada.* 1987.
Type-C print, 14.69 x 21.94 in., 37.31 x 55.73 cm.

PLATE 38
Len Jenshel, *Machias Maine.* 1993.
Type-C print, 14.75 x 21.81 in., 37.5 x 55.4 cm.

PLATE 41

Mark Klett, *Bullet-Riddled Saguaro Near Fountain Hills, 5/21/82.* 1982.
Silverprint, 16 x 20 in., 40.6 x 50.8 cm.

96

PLATE 42
Mark Klett, *Nuclear Generating Station, Palo Verde, 50 Miles from Phoenix, 1/4/86.* 1986.
Silverprint, 16 x 20 in., 40.6 x 50.8 cm.

PLATE 50
Richard Misrach, *Desert Fire #11.* 1985.
Dye coupler print, 18.25 x 23.12 in., 46.3 x 58.7 cm.

PLATE 55
Eric Paddock, *Hay Truck, Pueblo County, Colorado.* 1991.
Type-C print, 12.25 x 18 in., 31.1 x 45.7 cm.

110

PLATE 56
Eric Paddock, *Imploded Molasses Tank, Loveland, Colorado.* 1991.
Type-C print, 12.25 x 18 in., 31.1 x 45.7 cm.

111

John Pfahl, *Pink Rock Rectangle (Artpark, Lewiston, New York, August 1975).* 1975.
Dye transfer print, 14.25 x 18.12 in., 36.2 x 46 cm.

PLATE 58
John Pfahl, *Australian Pines (Fort DeSoto, Florida, February 1977).* 1977.
Dye transfer print, 14.19 x 18.12 in., 36 x 46 cm.

113

PLATE 59

Jim Sanborn, *Topographic Projection: Shiprock, New Mexico.* 1995.
Cibachrome print, 30 x 36 in., 76.2 x 91.4 cm.

114

PLATE 60
Jim Sanborn, *Implied Geometries: Notom, Utah.* 1995.
Cibachrome print, 23.75 x 30 in., 60.3 x 76.2 cm.

Outfall Drainage Ditch at Union Carbide Plant

What's in these ditches? A company just put in an application to the Texas Water Commission(TWC) to discharge 2.2 million gallons of wastewater a day into an unnamed roadside ditch which leads to Galveston Bay.

Rita Carlson

The Texas Water Commission and the U.S. Environmental Protection Agency have to find a balance of environmental and economic factors in the regulatory process.

John Ward, Water Quality Manager
Texas Water Commission, District 7

The TWC is charged to prevent pollution. That's what the Clean Water Act says to do. They do not prevent pollution, they permit pollution, taking on the notion that it must be balanced with economic development, and I agree with them...but, let's add in the true cost which is a reduced productive environment. It's a tremendous cost, a huge subsidy.

Brian Cain
Resource Contaminant Specialist
U.S. Fish and Wildlife Service

PLATE 61

Sharon Stewart, *Outfall Drainage Ditch at Union Carbide Plant*. 1989.
Silverprint, 19 x 14 in., 48.3 x 35.5 cm.

Chevron's 160 Acre Uranium Mill Tailings Pond
Contents: Six Million Tons of Radioactive Waste and Chemical Solvents

What we're concerned about is radioactive particles that go up and latch onto a particle of dust, or get into the water from underground. When you drink, eat, or breathe it, a certain kind of energy radiates in the body that nicks this cell, that cell, this cell again, until it is dead, changed, or growing.

Mike Trial, Co-Chair
Panna Maria Concerned Citizens

We contend that we have not damaged anyone, or will we in the future.

Kevin Raabe
Environmental/Safety Coordinator
Panna Maria Uranium Operations
Chevron Resources Company

PLATE 62

Sharon Stewart, *Chevron's 160 Acre Uranium Mill Tailings Pond, Contents: Six Million Tons of Radioactive Waste and Chemical Solvents.* 1989.
Silverprint, 19 x 14 in., 48.3 x 35.5 cm.

PLATE 63
Martin Stupich, *Phelps Dodge Copper Pit, Morenci, Arizona.* 1989.
Silverprint collage of four sections, 7.5 x 26 in., 19 x 66 cm.

PLATE 64

Martin Stupich, *Coolidge Dam from Spillway Platform, with San Carlos Reservoir.* 1989.

Silverprints (three-panel collage), each 22.25 x 10.75 in., 56.5 x 27.3 cm.

PLATE 65

Martin Stupich, *Con-Imperial Pit, Gold Hill, Nevada (Storey County).* 1982.
Silverprint, 9.1 x 36 in., 23.1 x 91.4 cm.

PLATE 66

Michelle Van Parys, *Tee Pee Rest Stop.* 1990.
Silverprint, 9 x 18 in., 22.9 x 45.7 cm.

he was a visiting professor of art history at the University of New Mexico. For the year 1996 he was awarded a Joshua C. Taylor Fellowship at the National Museum of American Art, Smithsonian Institution, Washington, D.C. Currently he is Curator of Photography at the High Museum of Art in Atlanta, Georgia.

He has organized numerous exhibitions with publications, including *Revealing Territory: Photographs of the Southwest,* by Mark Klett (1992); *Walker Evans and William Christenberry: Of Time and Place* (1990); and *Diane Arbus: Magazine Work* (1984). He is presently working on an exhibition and publication on John K. Hillers's photographs of the Pueblos in the 1870s and 1880s, *Reflecting Cultures: Photographs of Native Americans by John K. Hillers.*

BIOGRAPHIES OF THE ARTISTS

ROBERT ADAMS

Born: 1937, Orange, New Jersey

Robert Adams currently resides in Oregon. He has a Ph.D. in English from the University of Southern California. During his distinguished career he has received two NEA and two Guggenheim Fellowships. He was a MacArthur Foundation Award winner in 1994. Adams's photographs were part of the seminal *New Topographics* exhibit at George Eastman House in Rochester, New York, in 1975. His work hangs in museums and collections including, among others, the Metropolitan Museum of Art in New York, the Museums of Modern Art in New York and San Francisco, the National Gallery of Art in Washington, D.C., and the Victoria and Albert Museum in London. He has published eighteen books of and on photography, including such well-known publications as *Los Angeles Spring*; *From the Missouri West*; *The New West: Landscapes Along the Colorado Front Range*; *Beauty in Photography: Essays in Defense of Traditional Values*; *To Make It Home: Photographs of the American West*; *Listening to the River*; and most recently, *West from the Columbia*.

LEWIS BALTZ

Born: 1945, Newport Beach, California

Lewis Baltz received his B.A. degree from the San Francisco Art Institute and his M.A. degree from Claremont Graduate School, both in fine arts. He has received one Guggenheim and two NEA Fellowships, as well as the Charles Pratt Memorial Award. His books include *San Quentin Point*; *Nevada*; *The New Industrial Parks Near Irvine, California*; *Candlestick Point*; *Rule Without Exception*; and *Park City*, written with Gus Blaisdell. His work has appeared recently in the Musée d'Art Moderne de la Ville de Paris; the Stedelijk Museum, Amsterdam; the Centre Pompidou, Paris; and the New York Institute for Contemporary Art. Lewis Baltz currently lives in France, where he continues his work.

BARBARA BOSWORTH

Born: 1953, Cleveland, Ohio

Barbara Bosworth lives in Massachusetts and teaches at the Massachusetts College of Art in Boston. She has been awarded an Individual Artist's Fellowship from the New England Foundation for the Arts, as well as a Guggenheim Fellowship. Her work is in the permanent collections of the National Museum of American Art, the San Francisco Museum of Modern Art, the Houston Museum of Fine Arts, the Cleveland Museum of Art, and the Hallmark Collection. Her work has appeared in numerous publications, including the 1992 survey *Between Home and Heaven: Contemporary American Landscape Photography* and the exhibition catalog *Centric 29: Barbara Bosworth*. She cocurated with Laura McPhee the exhibition *The Country Between Us,* which originated at the Huntington Gallery of the Massachusetts College of Art.

MARILYN BRIDGES

Born: 1948, Allendale, New Jersey

Marilyn Bridges received her Master of Fine Arts degree from the Rochester Institute of Technology. She has been the recipient of a Guggenheim Fellowship, an NEA grant, and a Fulbright grant.

1991); *Stopping Time: A Rephotographic Survey of Lake Tahoe,* with essays by C. Elizabeth Raymond and Robert E. Blesse (Albuquerque: University of New Mexico Press, 1992); and *Humanature* (Austin: University of Texas Press, 1996). He served as editor of a fifth book, *Arid Waters: Photographs from the Water in the West Project* (Reno: University of Nevada Press, 1992). His photographs have been exhibited in more than fifty museums nationally and internationally and appear in the collections of the Museum of Modern Art in New York, the National Museum of American Art, the San Francisco Museum of Modern Art, the Amon Carter Museum, and the Los Angeles County Museum of Art. He is the recipient of two NEA fellowships. He lives with his family in Reno, Nevada.

EMMET GOWIN

Born: 1941, Danville, Virginia

Emmet Gowin graduated with a B.A. in graphic design from the Richmond Professional Institute (Virginia Commonwealth University) and received an M.F.A. in photography with Harry Callahan at the Rhode Island School of Design. He has been a recipient of a Guggenheim and two NEA fellowships; awards from the Southeastern Center for Contemporary Art and the Seattle Arts Commission; the 1983 Governor's Award for Excellence in the Arts from the State of Pennsylvania; the 1992 Friends of Photography Peer Award; and a Pew Fellowship in the Arts. Among his books and catalogs are *Emmet Gowin: Photographs*; *Petra: In the Hashemite Kingdom of Jordan*; and a 1990 retrospective of his work, *Emmet Gowin: Photography—This Vegetable Earth Is But a Shadow,* which was published by the Philadelphia Museum of Art. His work is in the collections of the Museum of Modern Art in New York, the Corcoran Gallery of Art, the Fogg Art Museum at Harvard, and the Philadelphia Museum of Art. He has been teaching in the Visual Arts Program at Princeton University since 1973.

WANDA HAMMERBECK

Born: 1945, Lincoln, Nebraska

Wanda Hammerbeck was educated at the University of North Carolina and Yale University. She also received an M.F.A. from the San Francisco Art Institute, where she was a Tiffany Fellow. She has been the recipient of three Photographer's Fellowships from the NEA. Her work has appeared in the books *Arid Waters: Photographs from the Water in the West Project*; *A River Too Far: The Past and Future of the Arid West*; *Nature Through Her Eyes*; *Western Waters*; and her monograph, *Depositions.* Her works are included in private and public collections, including the Fogg Art Museum of Harvard University, the Center for Creative Photography, the Houston Museum of Fine Arts, the Denver Art Museum, the Museum of Modern Art and the Metropolitan Museum of Art in New York, the Art Museum at Princeton University, the San Franciso Museum of Modern Art, and the Australian National Gallery.

TIMOTHY HEARSUM

Born: 1946, Dayton, Ohio

Timothy Hearsum received his bachelor's and master's degrees in fine arts from Ohio University and the State University of New York, Buffalo, respectively. His work hangs in over four hundred private, corporate, and public collections, including the Museums of Modern Art in New York and San Francisco, the International Museum of Photography, George Eastman House in Rochester, New York, the Chicago Institute of Design, and the Smithsonian Institution. He has participated in solo and group exhibitions, including those at the Oakland Museum, the San Diego Museum of Art, the Rochester Institute of Technology, and the Santa Barbara Museum of Art.

LEN JENSHEL

Born: 1949, Brooklyn, New York

Len Jenshel lives in New York. He received his degree from the Cooper Union. He has had solo exhibitions at the Art Institute of Chicago, the International Center for Photography in New York, the Yokohama Museum in Japan, and the Carnegie Institute, Pittsburgh, and his work has appeared in numerous group exhibitions. He is the recipient of an NEA and a Guggenheim Fellowship as well as a Graham Foundation grant. He has taught at various schools in New York, including the Cooper Union and New York University. His monographs include *Travels in the American West: Photographers at Work* and *Hot Spots: America's Volcanic Landscape,* which he published with his wife, Diane Cook. His work is in the collections of museums such as the Boston Museum of Fine Arts, the Houston Museum of Fine Arts, the Museum of Modern Art in New York, the National Museum of American Art, and the San Francisco Museum of Modern Art.

SANT KHALSA

Born: 1953, New York, New York

Sant Khalsa received her bachelor of fine arts degree from the Maryland Institute College of Art in Baltimore and her master of fine arts degree from California State University, Fullerton. She lives in Southern California, where she is a professor of art at California State University, San Bernardino. A major focus of her work has been to document photographically the changing course of the Santa Ana River, the interaction of humanity with the river, and the effects of industry and development on the river and its inhabitants. The Santa Ana River Project is part of the Water in the West Project. Her work has been shown nationally in numerous exhibitions and is collected by museums and universities, including the UCR California Museum of Photography in Riverside.

MARK KLETT

Born: 1952, Albany, New York

Following an undergraduate degree in geology, Mark Klett earned his master of fine arts degree from the State University of New York at Buffalo. Early in his career he worked with the U.S. Geological Survey. He is the recipient of three NEA Fellowships and won the Photographer of the Year Award from the Friends of Photography in 1992. His work has appeared in solo exhibitions at the National Museum of American Art, the Center for Creative Photography in Tucson, the Amon Carter Museum, the Los Angeles County Museum of Art, and the Art Institute in Chicago. He is the author or co-author of eight books, including *Second View: The Rephotographic Survey Project*; *Traces of Eden: Travels in the Desert Southwest*; *Revealing Territory: Photographs of the Southwest*; and *Desert Legends: Re-storying the Sonoran Borderlands,* which he co-authored with Gary Nabhan. His work appears in the collections of many museums and private collections, including the Art Institute of Chicago, the Museums of Modern Art in New York and San Francisco, the Victoria and Albert Museum in London, and the Whitney Museum of American Art.

GREG MacGREGOR

Born: 1941, La Crosse, Wisconsin

Greg MacGregor received a master of science degree in physics and worked for a time as an astrophysicist at Lawrence Radiation Laboratory. Later he obtained a second master's degree in photography from San Francisco State University. He has been actively photographing the Great Basin Desert for twenty-five years. His work appears in many collections, including the Museums of Modern Art in New York and San Francisco, the Houston Museum of Fine Arts, the Bibliothèque Nationale in Paris, the Oakland Museum, and the High Museum of Art in Atlanta. He is of Ben Glaha; *Arid Waters*; and *A River Too Far*. His work has been collected by the High Museum of Art in Atlanta, the Library of Congress, the National Archives, the National Museum of American Art, and other museums and corporate collections.

MICHELLE VAN PARYS

Born: 1957, Arlington, Virginia

Michelle Van Parys received degrees in art from the Corcoran School of Art and Virginia Commonwealth University in Richmond, Virginia. She currently lives in Charleston, South Carolina, and teaches photography at the College of Charleston. Her work appears in a number of collections, including those of the San Francisco Museum of Modern Art and the Virginia Museum of Fine Arts. She was a co-author of the books *Hoaxes, Humbugs, and Spectacles* and *Dear Mr. Ripley: A Compendium of Curioddities from the Believe It or Not! Archive*.

CATHERINE WAGNER

Born: 1953, San Francisco, California

Catherine Wagner was educated in art at San Francisco State University, where she received her M.A. degree. She has also received two fellowships from the NEA as well as a Guggenheim Fellowship and an Aaron Siskind Fellowship. Her work has been collected by such museums as the Metropolitan Museum of Art and the Museum of Modern Art in New York, the San Francisco Museum of Modern Art, the Bibliothèque Nationale de Paris, the Oakland Museum, the Museum of Fine Arts in Houston, the Los Angeles County Museum of Art, and the Victoria and Albert Museum in London. Her work has appeared in many publications, including the monographs *American Classroom: The Photographs of Catherine Wagner* and *Home and Other Stories: Photographs by Catherine Wagner*; and the catalogs *Catherine Wagner* and *Changing Places: Photographs by Catherine Wagner*. Wagner's most recent publication is *Art & Science: Investigating Matter, Photographs by Catherine Wagner*. She is a professor of art at Mills College in Oakland.

EDWARD WESTON

Born: 1886, Highland Park, Illinois

Died: 1958, Carmel, California

Weston moved to California in 1906 to become a portrait photographer. Although he built a successful studio in Tropico, California, he became interested in abstraction and traveled to New York, where he met Alfred Stieglitz and Charles Sheeler. In 1923 he began to spend time in Mexico, where he was involved with the famous painters of the Mexican Renaissance. He both influenced and was influenced by the likes of Diego Rivera, José Clemente Orozco, and David Alfaro Siqueiros. In 1929 he established his studio in Carmel, California, and in 1932 he founded Group f/64, the group of photographers who championed "straight" photography. He was the first photographer to be awarded a Guggenheim Fellowship. He had a profound influence on photographic art both through Group f/64 and individually. His work is represented in the collections of every major museum. His diaries, *The Daybooks of Edward Weston,* describe the development of his thought. His work is memorialized in many books, including *Supreme Instants: The Photography of Edward Weston*; *Edward Weston: The Flame of Recognition—His Photographs*; *Edward Weston: Forms of Passion*; and *Edward Weston: Fifty Years—The Definitive Volume of His Photographic Work*.

SUGGESTED READINGS

Adams, Ansel. *Examples: The Making of 40 Photographs.* Boston: Little, Brown, 1983.

Adams, Robert. *The Architecture and Art of Early Hispanic Colorado.* Boulder: Colorado Associated University Press, 1974.

——. *Beauty in Photography: Essays in Defense of Traditional Values.* Millerton, N.Y.: Aperture, 1981.

——. *Denver: A Photographic Survey of the Metropolitan Area.* Boulder: Colorado Associated University Press, 1977.

——. *From the Missouri West.* New York: Aperture, 1980.

——. *Listening to the River.* New York: Aperture, 1994.

——. *Los Angeles Spring.* New York: Aperture, 1986.

——. *The New West: Landscapes Along the Colorado Front Range.* Boulder: University of Colorado Press, 1975.

——. *Our Lives and Our Children: Photographs Taken Near the Rocky Flats Nuclear Weapons Plant.* New York: Aperture, 1983.

——. *Perfect Times, Perfect Places.* New York: Aperture, 1988.

——. *Prairie: Photographs by Robert Adams.* Denver: Denver Art Museum, 1978.

——. *Summer Nights.* New York: Aperture, 1985.

——. *To Make It Home: Photographs of the American West.* New York: Aperture, 1989.

——. *West from the Columbia.* New York: Aperture, 1995.

——. *White Churches of the Plains: Examples from Colorado.* Boulder: Colorado Associated University Press, 1970.

——. *Why People Photograph.* New York: Aperture, 1994.

Bakely, Donald C. *If: A Big Word with the Poor.* Photographs by Terry Evans. Newton, Kans.: Faith and Life Press, 1976.

Baltz, Lewis. *Candlestick Point.* Essay by Gus Blaisdell. Tokyo: Gallery Min, 1989.

——. *Maryland.* Essay by Jane Livingston. Washington, D.C.: Corcoran Gallery of Art, 1976.

——. *Nevada.* New York: Castelli Graphics, 1978.

——. *The New Industrial Parks Near Irvine, California.* New York: Castelli Graphics, 1974.

——. *Rule Without Exception.* Edited by Julia Brown Turrell. Albuquerque: University of New Mexico Press, 1991.

——. *San Quentin Point.* Essay by Mark Haworth-Booth. New York: Aperture, 1996.

——, and Gus Blaisdell. *Park City.* Millerton, N.Y.: Artspace Press, 1980.

Bosworth, Barbara. *Centric 29: Barbara Bosworth.* Essay by Sheryl Conkelton. Los Angeles: Los Angeles County Museum of Art, 1987.

Bridges, Marilyn. *Egypt: Antiquities from Above.* Boston: Little, Brown, 1996.

——. *Markings: Aerial Views of Sacred Landscapes.* Preface by Haven O'More; essays by Maria Reiche et al.; afterword by Marilyn Bridges. New York: Aperture, 1986.

——. *Planet Peru: An Aerial Journey Through a Timeless Land.* New York: Aperture, 1991.

——. *The Sacred and Secular: A Decade of Aerial Photography.* New York: International Center of Photography, 1990.

——. *Vue d'Oiseau: La Mission Photographie Transmanche.* Douchy: Centre Regional de la Photographie, 1996.

Bunnell, Peter C. *Emmet Gowin: Photographs, 1966–1983.* Washington, D.C.: The Gallery, 1983.

——, and David Featherstone, eds. *EW 100: Centennial Essays in Honor of Edward Weston.* Carmel: Friends of Photography, 1986.

Cahn, Robert, and Robert Glenn Ketchum. *American Photographers and the National Parks.* New York: Viking Press, 1981.

Conger, Amy. *Edward Weston in Mexico, 1923–1926.* Foreword by Van Deren Coke. Albuquerque: University of New Mexico Press, 1983.

Conkelton, Sheryl. *Home and Other Stories: Photographs by Catherine Wagner.* Essay by Anne Lamott. Albuquerque: University of New Mexico Press, 1993.

Current, Karen. *Photographs and the Old West.* Photos selected and printed by William R. Current. Edited by Margaret L. Kaplan and Ellen Shultz. New York: Abrams, 1978.

Dawson, Robert. *Robert Dawson Photographs.* Tokyo: Gallery Min, 1988.

Deal, Joe. *Joe Deal.* Albuquerque: University of New Mexico Press, 1992.

——. *Southern California Photographs, 1976–1986.* Essays by Mark Johnstone and Edward Leffingwell. Albuquerque: University of New Mexico Press, 1992.

Del Tredici, Robert. *At Work in the Fields of the Bomb.* Introduction by Jonathan Schell. New York: Perennial Library, 1987.

——. *Closing the Circle on the Splitting of the Atom.* Introduction by Jonathan Schell. Washington, D.C.: U.S. Department of Energy, 1995.

Snyder, Joel. *American Frontiers: The Photographs of Timothy H. O'Sullivan, 1867–1874*. Millerton, N.Y.: Aperture, 1981.

Stegner, Wallace. *The American West as Living Space*. Ann Arbor: University of Michigan Press, 1987.

Stephens, Hal G., and Eugene M. Shoemaker. *In the Footsteps of John Wesley Powell: An Album of Comparative Photographs of the Green and Colorado Rivers, 1871–72 and 1968*. Boulder and Denver: Johnson Books and Powell Society, 1987.

Sternfeld, Joel. *American Prospects: Photographs*. Introduction by Andy Grunberg; afterword by Anne W. Tucker. New York: Times Books, 1987.

Stewart, Sharon. *Toxic Tour of Texas*. Austin: State of Texas General Land Office and Texas Photographic Society, 1992.

Swimme, Brian, and Thomas Berry. *The Universe Story: From the Primordial Flaring Forth to the Ecozoic Era—A Celebration of the Unfolding of the Cosmos*. San Francisco: Harper/San Francisco, 1992.

Tice, George A. *Hometowns: An American Pilgrimage*. Boston: Little, Brown, 1988.

Tucker, Anne Wilkes. *American Classroom: The Photographs of Catherine Wagner*. Essay by Willie Morris. New York: Aperture, 1988.

——. *Crimes and Splendors: The Desert Cantos of Richard Misrach*. Essay by Rebecca Solnit. Boston: Bulfinch Press, 1996.

Vroman, A. C. *Photographer of the Southwest: Adam Clark Vroman, 1856–1916*. Edited by Ruth I. Mahood and Robert A. Weinstein; introduction by Beaumont Newhall. Los Angeles: Ward Ritchie Press, 1961.

Wagner, Catherine. *Art & Science: Investigating Matter, Photographs by Catherine Wagner*. Text by Cornelia Homburg, William Gass, and Helen F. Longino. Munich: Nazraeli Press, 1996.

——. *Catherine Wagner*. Tokyo: Gallery Min, 1987.

——. *Changing Places: Photographs by Catherine Wagner*. Houston: Farish Gallery, Rice University, 1990.

——. *Places: Photographs by Catherine Wagner*. Houston: Farish Gallery, Rice University, 1990.

Watkins, Carleton Emmons. *Carleton E. Watkins: Photographs, 1861–1874*. Essay by Peter E. Palmquist. San Francisco: Fraenkel Gallery in association with Bedford Arts, 1989.

——. *Photographs of the Columbia River and Oregon*. Edited by James Alinder; essays by David Featherstone and Russ Anderson. Carmel: Friends of Photography and Weston Gallery, 1979.

——. *Carleton E. Watkins: Selected Texts and Bibliography*. Edited by Amy Rule. Boston: G. K. Hall, 1993.

Weston, Edward. *The Daybooks of Edward Weston*. Edited by Nancy Newhall. 2 vols. Millerton, N.Y.: Aperture, 1973.

White, Minor. *Minor White: Rites and Passages—His Photographs Accompanied by Excerpts from His Diaries and Letters*. Biographical essay by James Baker Hall. Millerton, N.Y.: Aperture, 1978.

William, Geoff. *Hidden Rainforests: Subtropical Rainforests and the Invertebrate Biodiversity*. Including photographs by Terry Evans. Kensington, Australia: New South Wales University Press, 1993.

Wilson, Alexander. *The Culture of Nature: North American Landscape from Disney to the Exxon Valdez*. Cambridge: Blackwell, 1992.

Wolf, Daniel. *American Space: Meaning in Nineteenth-Century Landscape Photography*. Middletown: Wesleyan University Press, 1983.

CREDITS

Ansel Adams, *Clearing Winter Storm, Yosemite National Park, California.* Copyright © 1991 by the Trustees of the Ansel Adams Publishing Rights Trust. Reproduced with the permission of the Trustees of the Ansel Adams Publishing Rights Trust.

Moonrise, Hernandez, New Mexico. Copyright © 1991 by the Trustees of the Ansel Adams Publishing Rights Trust. Reproduced with the permission of the Trustees of the Ansel Adams Publishing Rights Trust.

Winter Sunrise, Sierra Nevada, from Lone Pine, California. Copyright © 1991 by the Trustees of the Ansel Adams Publishing Rights Trust. Reproduced with the permission of the Ansel Adams Publishing Rights Trust.

Robert Adams, *Burning Oil Sludge, Boulder County, Colorado.* Copyright © by Robert Adams.

Colorado Springs, Colorado. Copyright © by Robert Adams.

Dead Palms Partially Uprooted, Ontario, California. Copyright © by Robert Adams.

North from Flagstaff Mountain, Boulder County, Colorado. Copyright © by Robert Adams.

Quarried Mesa Top, Pueblo County, Colorado. Copyright © by Robert Adams.

Lewis Baltz, *The Nevada Portfolio.* Copyright © by Lewis Baltz.

Albert Bierstadt, *Sunrise, Yosemite Valley.* Reproduced with the permission of the Amon Carter Museum, Fort Worth, Texas.

Sunset in the Yosemite Valley. Reproduced with the permission of the Pioneer Museum and Haggin Galleries, Haggin Museum, Stockton, California.

Barbara Bosworth, *Moose Meat, Pittsburgh, New Hampshire.* Copyright © by Barbara Bosworth.

Nate, Skinning Day, Moosehead Lake, Maine. Copyright © by Barbara Bosworth.

Marilyn Bridges, *Blythe Site #2, Blythe, California.* Copyright © by Marilyn Bridges.

Highway Emerging, Nevada. Copyright © by Marilyn Bridges.

Parker Rattlesnake, Arizona. Copyright © by Marilyn Bridges.

Winterhaven-Stickman, California. Copyright © by Marilyn Bridges.

Frederick Edwin Church, *The Icebergs.* Copyright © Dallas Museum of Art. Reproduced with the permission of the Dallas Museum of Art.

Dawn-Starr Crowther, *Autograph Tree (Bearing Witness), Nani Man Gardens, Hawaii.* Copyright © by Dawn-Starr Crowther.

Robert Dawson, *Clear Cutting Slopes, Klamath River Basin, California.* Copyright © by Robert Dawson.

Oildale, California. Copyright © by Robert Dawson.

Plow Patterns and Power Poles, Sherman Island, California. Copyright © by Robert Dawson.

Polluted New River, Calexico, Mexican American Border, California. Copyright © by Robert Dawson.

Private Property, Lake Tahoe, California. Copyright © by Robert Dawson.

San Francisco's Entire Water Supply Flows Through This Pipe, Near Mather, California. Copyright © by Robert Dawson.

San Luis Drain, Kesterson National Wildlife Refuge, California. Copyright © by Robert Dawson.

Joe Deal, *Duplex Dividing Wall, Anaheim Hills, California.* Copyright © by Joe Deal.

Retreat, Upland, California. Copyright © by Joe Deal.

Santa Ana Winds, Riverside, California. Copyright © by Joe Deal.

Sunset Beach, California. Copyright © by Joe Deal.

Robert Del Tredici, *Industrial Safety Sign (Area 5, Nevada Test Site, Mercury, Nevada, July 1983).* Copyright © by Robert Del Tredici.

Tending to Misty Rain (Area 12, Nevada Test Site, Nye County, Nevada, October 29, 1984). Copyright © by Robert Del Tredici.

Terry Evans, *Haystacks, South Central Nebraska.* Copyright © by Terry Evans.